The Potter's Wheel

Dear Mary Lou & Lee,
May God's Hands
Enfold
You

Love,
Clay

Gracious and loving God,
as we journey through these holy seasons,
give us, we pray,
the courage to come face to face with ourselves
and the hope to know that you are continuously shaping us
into the persons you created us to be,
as we follow the example of life which you have given us
in Jesus Christ our Lord and Savior.

AMEN

The Potter's Wheel

Selected Sermons through the Cycle of the Liturgical Year

THE REVEREND DR. CLAY H. TURNER

From the pulpit of
The Episcopal Church of the Advent
Spartanburg, South Carolina
1990–2004

THE ADVENT FOUNDATION
The Episcopal Church of the Advent
Spartanburg, South Carolina
2006

ISBN-10: 0-87152-553-4
ISBN-13: 978-0-87152-553-6
Library of Congress Control Number: 2006935821
Manufactured in the United States of America

The paper used in this publication meets the minimum requirements of
American National Standard for Information Science—Permanence of Paper
for Printed Library Materials, ANSI Z39.48-1984.

Publication arrangements by
THE REPRINT COMPANY, PUBLISHERS
Spartanburg, South Carolina

Dedication

It is my joy and privilege to dedicate this book to the beloved
members of The Episcopal Church of the Advent,
who inspired and encouraged me,
who faithfully listened,
and who gracefully and courageously responded to
God's call.

Contents

Foreword—The Right Reverend Bennett J. Sims . . . . *xi*

Foreword—The Reverend John Westerhoff . . . . *xiii*

Preface . . . . *xvii*

Acknowledgments . . . . *xix*

The Potter's Wheel . . . . *xxi*

ADVENT *1*

Disburb Us, Lord *3*

Now Is the Time 7

Are You Ready for Christmas Yet? *12*

Stir Up Sunday *18*

Two Things, and That's All *24*

Pieces of Clay *31*

CHRISTMASTIDE *33*

All I Want for Christmas *35*

Hearts a-Bustin' with Love *40*

Tinsel on the Tree *46*

Practicing God's Goodness *50*

Pieces of Clay *57*

EPIPHANY 59

When the Wine Runs Out 61

Healers in a Hate-Torn World 66

Inside Out 70

Something Old, Something New 75

A Person-to-Person Call 80

The Growing Season 85

Pieces of Clay 93

LENT 95

A Pruning and Thinning Time 97

Because Jesus Wept 103

All You (N)ever Needed 111

For Her, I Will Do Anything 117

The Robins Are Back 122

Pieces of Clay 129

EASTERTIDE 131

Five Little Words 133

A Great Fish Story 138

Mixed Emotions 144

All Locked Up 151

Breaking the News 157

Pieces of Clay 163

PENTECOST *165*

May I Light Your Lamp? *167*

First Impressions *173*

As Sheep Among Wolves *179*

Life Is Not Fair *185*

Praying for Rain *188*

Just Who Do You Think You Are? *196*

Living through the Worst of Times 201

Loved into Being 206

A Ladder and a Lantern 212

Good-bye and Hello, June 6, 2004 .... *219*

Now and Forever, June 27, 2004 224

Pieces of Clay 229

Afterword *231*

*F*oreword

BENNETT J. SIMS
Bishop Emeritus, the Episcopal Diocese of Atlanta
Founder, the Institute for Servant Leadership
2004

Clay Howard Turner earned the highest distinction that is in the power of a parish priest to achieve. *He won and held the hearts of his people*. What this means is that Clay has been singularly obedient to the highest law of life, as articulated by an earlier saint, that "love is the fulfilling of the law" (ROMANS 13:10).

Other attributes in his character are worthy of distinction. One of them is his gracious intellect. Clay graduated magna cum laude from the Duke Divinity School in 1964, and in 1991, while serving as rector of a large urban church, he earned the doctor of ministry degree from Princeton Theological Seminary. Adding even more to his stature as a priest is his record of leadership in service to the several communities of his ministry in Virginia and the Carolinas—preeminently in his final parish before retirement, The Church of the Advent in Spartanburg, South Carolina. There he initiated the St. Luke's Free Medical Clinic, was co-chair of the Stop the Violence Collaboration, served on the boards of numerous community organizations, and was voted Citizen of the Year by several civic groups.

The catalogue of Clay's achievements in community servant-hood is but a distillation of his many credits of outreach. More to the point of his servant leadership are his gifts of moving and shaking a fairly conservative parish church into an enlarged and liberal vision of Christian commitment and generosity.

The Church of the Advent has grown far beyond its earlier boundaries of self-understanding since he became their rector in 1990. He has led the parish in community distinction with his voice as their preacher and with his compassion and skill as a pastoral counselor. He has done this as a lifelong learner. He seems to know that in the Native American Iroquios language there is no word for "teach," but thirty-five terms for "learn." In support of this assumption it is well known that Clay refuses to freeze his sermon manuscripts and notes in a file cabinet. They are nowhere in storage except for the taped records from which the content of this book is fashioned. Outside the pulpit and the lecture platform (from which he has recently delivered talks to community groups on such conservationists as Johnny Appleseed and Aldo Leopold) he pursues fresh learning with a passion for what is yet unlearned. Coincident with his retirement, he has begun the process of memorizing the scholarly Latin names of the plants and insects of his abiding interest as a gardener and conservationist.

I have known Clay since his days as rector of St. John's Episcopal Church in Roanoke, Virginia, where he served for fifteen years before coming to Spartanburg. He has been a servant leader of velvet and steel in all places of his wide ministry. I join with all who have known and loved him in a resounding salute to his stirring gift of gentle persuasion.

Foreword

JOHN WESTERHOFF
Episcopal priest, former professor of theology, Duke University
Theologian-in-residence, St. Luke's Episcopal Church, Atlanta
2004

In the Episcopal Church's *Book of Common Prayer*, there is "an examination of candidates for ordination to the priesthood." It makes clear that all the baptized are called to ministry—to the service of God in every moment of every day, in everything we do—but some are called by the church to be "pastors, priests, and teachers."

Pastors—"to love and serve the people among whom they work, caring alike for young and old, strong and weak, rich and poor."

Priests—"to declare God's forgiveness to penitent sinners, to pronounce God's blessing, to share in the administration of Holy Baptism, and in the celebration of the mystery of Christ's Body and Blood."

Teachers—"to proclaim by word and deed the Gospel of Jesus Christ" (which is, interestingly, what it also means to preach).

Clay Turner has exemplified throughout his life and work this image of the priesthood. From all I can discern, Clay has lived with a theology of relationships. That is, the Christian life of faith has to do with our relationship with God, with our true selves in the image of God, all people, and nature. The moral life is neither to turn everything over to God, nor to assume responsibility for everything ourselves. We are to acknowledge that we are not in control of anything. We are, by nature, absolutely dependent on God. And, importantly, God has chosen to be dependent on us. We are to live an interdependent life of cooperation with God, which necessitates a strong spiritual life—a life devoted to an ever-deepening and loving relationship with God.

My evidence is that Clay knew that if the church was to be the Body of Christ—God's reconciling presence in the world—it had to be a community of faith, a family in which God's reconciling power was made known, living and active in the lives of the people. Knowing that it was not enough to believe the truth—we must "do the truth"—he was still devoted to engaging in learning before taking actions, to being before doing. Combining prayer with preaching that was teaching and teaching that was preaching, his priesthood was undergirded by the fact that he chose to be a shepherd, attentive to his flock. While he gave himself to the larger church and society, his greatest satisfaction was staying at home and caring for his people, a flock who, therefore, knew his voice.

A talented communicator, he will be remembered as a faithful preacher who understood what it meant to provide a sermon (from the Latin for conversation) or homily (from the Greek for conversation) for his people that would nurture and nourish them for the Christian life of faith.

Now published, the sermons of Clay Turner are a tribute to his life and work at The Episcopal Church of the Advent. Long-time parishioners will read them and be helped to remember their journey through the years. New parishioners will read them to better understand why The Church of the Advent lives as it does. For others, the book will be a useful means for coming to know a beloved priest of a healthy parish.

To be a rector of a parish for fourteen years and be loved still is a tremendous achievement—of course, with God's help—as well as a testimony of Clay's understanding of leadership. As he and The Church of the Advent go their separate ways, his spirit will remain. But reading the sermons in this book will help free the congregation to move on to love a new rector as it continues its journey to be open to the Spirit and faithful to its calling. Thanks be to God.

*P*reface

I was overwhelmed with gratitude when, at my retirement celebration on the last Sunday of June 2004, the congregation of The Episcopal Church of the Advent presented me with many wonderful accolades and gifts, among them being the surprising announcement of plans to publish my sermons.

This proved to be a daunting task, since I never preached from manuscripts, and there were no notes of my sermons. However, since 1995 there had been tape recordings of most of my sermons. Unbeknownst to me, my devoted secretary, Mary Mills, spent hundreds of hours at home diligently transcribing spoken words into a printed text. This tremendous effort on her part was the beginning of this creative process.

I have chosen to preserve in this book a variety of sermons, which I believe are some of my more effective efforts at interpreting the Gospel for a particular time, place, and people. Many of them are directly connected to pivotal events in the life of the parish. I hope my readers will use these insights to strengthen them in their spiritual journeys and to give them courage to live their lives to the fullest as God's gifts to the world.

The title, *The Potter's Wheel*, was chosen by those people who developed this idea and whose vision inspired it. I shall attempt to apply the metaphor of the potter as a way of dividing the selected sermons into the structure of the liturgical year.

In order for the pottery experience to be successful, a definite procedure must be followed. The first step is to awaken a dormant lump of raw clay and prepare it for throwing by kneading or wedging it to make it pliable and receptive to the potter's design.

Then the lump is thrown onto the wheel and formed into a symmetrical shape in a step called centering. Next the lump is opened up so that it may be shaped according to the vision of the potter. When the freshly formed pot has air-dried, it is placed in intense heat in a kiln. During this first bisque firing all of the moisture and impurities are burned away. The pot is now ready to be covered with a bright, beautiful coating called a glaze. The actual color of the finished vessel is not visible until it has been fired a second time. After being transformed with new color and brilliance, the glazed pot is put to use in a way that serves the purpose of those who possess it.

I have discovered throughout the duration of my ministry that the process of our spiritual formation is similar to the process of shaping a pot. The liturgical year traces this development of our souls in a most meaningful way. God is the potter, we are the clay, and the parish is the wheel that shapes, refines, and energizes us to become God's extension of his love into the world. These sermons are the product of the inspiration of a wonderful congregation as it placed itself in God's hands to be formed by his love.

Clay H. Turner

Acknowledgments

Where does one begin? I should begin by expressing my heartfelt gratitude to all those people who called me into being and loved me into life. I thank those who shared their wisdom, values, passions, and struggles to shape me into the person, the parson, the priest I have become. Much of this development happened through the four wonderful congregations I was blessed to serve, who lovingly and patiently shared their spiritual journeys with me: from Christ Church in Rocky Mount, North Carolina, to Trinity Church in Statesville, North Carolina, to St. John's in Roanoke, Virginia, and finally to The Church of the Advent, Spartanburg, South Carolina.

Above all, I am grateful to Jane Rollins Turner, my stalwart companion, without whose steady support, constant encouragement, and self-giving partnership my ministry would never have developed.

My extreme gratitude goes to Keith, our son, whose boundless creativity, keen sensitivity, penetrating insight, and ability as a wordsmith refined the selection process and improved my conversational style.

My heartfelt thanks to Nancy Ruth Patterson, noted author of children's literature and teacher of creative writing, long-time friend and fellow traveler, who was the midwife for this project, without whose creative wisdom, great exuberance, hopeful guidance, and plain old good cheer this book would not have been brought into being. She helped us shape a huge body of material into a readable form without losing my voice in the process.

Last, but certainly not least, I want to express my apprecia-tion to members of The Church of the Advent, specifically Susu Johnson and Martha Blackman, who originated the idea of pub-lishing my sermons as a part of the celebration of my retirement. This committee planted the seed, arranged for the transcription from tapes, read and edited, and suggested the title for this vol-ume. In particular, thanks to Tom Smith, whose calm, steady guidance and constant striving for excellence called us to develop the best possible outcome in this and many other endeavors.

—

The heresies, errors of judgment, and theological shortsighted-ness are mine to claim. The conversations used in my sermons are obviously paraphrased. If the reader finds any comforting wisdom in these pages, people who have entrusted me into their lives and allowed me to walk this journey of faith with them have passed it on to me. To all of them I am truly grateful for forty years of wonder-full and joy-full living.

The Potter's Wheel

The Episcopal Church of the Advent, founded in 1848, is a downtown church in Spartanburg, South Carolina (population approximately forty thousand). Historically, among its parishioners have been leaders in business, politics, and community organizations. Into this congregation came Clay Turner in the fall of 1990.

By the time he retired in the summer of 2004, "his people" had become part of the initiation of The St. Luke's Free Clinic for the working uninsured; continued sending youth and adults on mission trips including working with the Lakota Sioux Indians in White Horse, South Dakota; adopted a low-achieving inner city school, becoming room mothers, tutors, and teacher's aides; co-chaired a Stop the Violence Collaboration after a random shooting; involved themselves in relief work at Ground Zero; and in a variety of other ways integrated themselves into the core of Spartanburg in "off the beaten path" ways.

Clay Turner counseled countless people, both members and nonmembers, making the church truly open to the community. He strengthened some marriages, saved others, and comforted the bereaved, the divorced, and the alienated.

He taught the church about servanthood ministry and challenged parishioners to be servant leaders—and taught best by the example of his own life. He truly molded the parish into a more energetic, compassionate, and active body, which produced a huge and positive impact on the Spartanburg community.

He made Advent better than it had been and, like the potter with his clay, better than the church knew it could be. A large part of this congregation has been turned by Clay Turner and come off his wheel newly created people committed to service to others and devoted to God.

Read, then, and enjoy *The Potter's Wheel*.

The Episcopal Church of the Advent
Spartanburg, South Carolina

Advent

Advent is the season of preparation, of making our spirits receptive and responsive to God's presence in our lives. As the potter kneads the clay to make it responsive to her or his centering touch, Advent softens and makes pliable our souls to receive the form of God's love in the incarnation.

PRAYER FOR ADVENT: Gracious Lord God, we watch, we wait, we look, we long for you. Dispel, we pray, the clouds and darkness of our life and awaken us to your presence, that we may walk in your light and your joy, through the power of the One who came to show us the way, your Son Jesus, our Savior and our Guide. AMEN

Disturb Us, Lord

MATTHEW 26:36–46

Then Jesus went with them to a place called Gethsemane; and he said to his disciples, "Sit here while I go over there and pray." He took with him Peter and the two sons of Zebedee, and began to be grieved and agitated. Then he said to them, "I am deeply grieved, even to death; remain here, and stay awake with me." And going a little farther, he threw himself on the ground and prayed, "My Father, if it is possible, let this cup pass from me; yet not what I want but what you want." Then he came to the disciples and found them sleeping; and he said to Peter, "So, could you not stay awake with me one hour? Stay awake and pray that you may not come into the time of trial; the spirit indeed is willing, but the flesh is weak." Again he went away for the second time and prayed, "My Father, if this cup cannot pass unless I drink it, your will be done." Again he came and found them sleeping, for their eyes were heavy. So leaving them again, he went away and prayed for the third time, saying the same words. Then he came to the disciples and said to them, "Are you still sleeping and taking your rest? See, the hour is at hand, and the Son of Man is betrayed into the hands of sinners. Get up, let us be going. See, my betrayer is at hand."

Accountability and choices. The necessity of having a vision for life, and faithfulness to that vision. All of these concepts constitute the core meaning of this gospel reading provided for our reflection today. And it's a perfect setting; it's perfect because we are in the midst of Christ the King Sunday. This is the day when we come face to face with our own accountability, our own choices. What is the vision which guides us in our living, and how faithful are we to the vision we have? Christ the King Sunday is our way of recognizing that our Lord is the King of our entire life. It is a launching pad for us to embark upon what is the most pivotal day in the entire history of this congregation.

Now why do I say that? If you were in the parish hall at ten o'clock this morning, you had a glimpse of why. We are at a point when we respond to the vision which God holds out before us—one that is going to present us with terrific challenges and hard choices as we anticipate some exciting possibilities we have never had before as a people.

The leaders of this parish have already presented a sharpened vision of what we have forged together out of three thousand hours of conversation and more than one hundred meetings over the last year. When we began this journey well over twelve months ago, your vestry and I were intentional to have this be a spiritual journey. We did several things intentionally to live out that vision. Every gathering was begun with a prayer asking God's guidance on what would happen there, and every gathering was closed with a prayer for God's blessing upon whatever had occurred. We also began each time of reflection out of a scriptural base as we began to hold up our vision of the people God was calling us to be in this time and in this place. Now we have a vision that is clear, a vision that is challenging, a vision that to some of us is frightening and to some of us is exhilarating. But nevertheless, we are now held accountable for how faithful we will be to the vision that we have before us.

We have been beneficiaries of so much given to us by those who have gone before us. Today we face the challenge of becoming benefactors to those who will come after us. In that challenge each of us will have to do some soul searching about how faithful we are going to be to the vision that God is placing before us.

You received a letter from me and our wardens outlining some of the steps we will take together as we go into our future, some of the things that will have to be changed about our life, some of the things that will remain constant, some of the things that we will be envisioning that have never happened here before. We have a wondrous year before us. We begin the season of New Year next Sunday on the first Sunday of Advent. What a wonderful time to move out of Christ the King Sunday into a whole new sense of beginning together as we make some bold new steps into our future. We are that future, and God has gifted us with unimaginable gifts and resources.

I am exhilarated by the challenges which lie before us because I know that we as the people of the Advent are a people of miraculous expectations. It is this strong sense, this strong faith I have in us, that enables me to face the challenge with a renewed sense of vigor and commitment as we all seek together to become the people who live under Christ's kingship in this place.

As we take these next steps together, it is appropriate that we hear again the prayer that I shared with you some months ago as we closed the Epiphany Project. It is a poem which has been passed down through history, one which guided the brave naval officer and explorer Sir Francis Drake to take risks and to move into uncharted waters and explore unknown territories. As he took those risks with his own fears and his own enthusiasms, this was the prayer that guided him, and I hope it will be the prayer that will guide us as we move into our future together.

Disturb us, Lord, when we are too pleased with ourselves;
When our dreams have become true because we dreamed too little.
When we arrived safely because we sailed too closely to the shore.

Disturb us, Lord, when with the abundance of things we possess we
     have lost our thirst for the waters of life;
Having fallen in love with life, we have ceased to dream of eternity.
And in our efforts to build a new earth, we have allowed our vision
     of the new heaven to dim.

Disturb us, Lord, to dare more boldly;
To venture on wider seas where storms will show your mastery;
Where losing sight of land, we shall find the stars.
We ask you to push back the horizons of our hopes,
And to push us into the future with strength, courage, vision, and love.
This we ask, in the name of our Captain, Jesus Christ.
Amen.

Now Is the Time

MARK 13:24–27

"But in those days, after that suffering, the sun will be darkened, and the moon will not give its light, and the stars will be falling from heaven, and the powers in the heavens will be shaken. Then they will see 'the Son of Man coming in clouds' with great power and glory. Then he will send out the angels, and gather his elect from the four winds, from the ends of the earth to the ends of heaven…"

Happy New Year!

Yes, I know it's only November, but in the church, it *is* a Happy New Year. It seems like only yesterday that we had finished lighting the four candles of Advent last year, and now we are beginning a new Advent season all over again.

This awareness in me has created a new awareness of what Advent can mean for each of us:

A sense of the shortness of life.

A sense of time's rapid passage.

The awareness that children grow from babes in arms to toddlers, to teenagers, to college graduates, and to new husbands and wives in a heartbeat.

A sense of life's slipping by us so quickly that we are not even aware of its passing.

The first Sunday of Advent says, "Be careful; be watchful; be awake; and be alert. Do not assume that you are going to have unlimited time in your future. *Now* is the time!"

Advent is a sober reminder of a fact that we all live with every day—the rapid passage of our time and the crucial importance of the present moment.

My Name is Asher Lev, a wonderful novel written by a Jewish author, Chaim Potok, speaks to the passage of time. The narrator, a painter, tells of a childhood memory that emerged as if by surprise on canvas. On a cold day, the painter as a six-year-old walked down the street hand in hand with his father. As they stood at a street corner, the little boy looked down in the gutter and saw a bird lying on its back.

"Is it dead, Papa?" he asked.

"Yes," his father said in a sad and distant way.

"Why did it die?"

"Everything that lives must die."

"Everything?"

"Yes."

"You, too, Papa? And Mama?"

"Yes."

"And me?"

"Yes."

"Why?"

"So life will be precious, Asher," the father said gently. "Something that is yours forever is *never* precious."

Something that is yours forever is never precious.

The first Sunday of Advent, this New Year's Day, reminds us of this fact. We are not given unlimited time, and we are not quite sure when the end of our time will come. No one has that knowledge. "I don't even know that for myself," our Lord once said.

But one day the end of time will come for us all. Right now the present moment is all we have. This is what this New Year's Day says to us in the life of the church:

Be awake.

Be alert.

Be watchful.

Be careful.

Take heed.

And be aware of the shortness and uncertainty of our human life.

Elisabeth Kübler-Ross, a psychiatrist from whom I have learned a lot, started her work at the University of Chicago about the time I began as a hospital chaplain at the Duke Medical Center in 1961. Through her insightful book *On Death and Dying*, she has taught us over the years the importance of listening to dying people…because dying people can have a lot to teach us about the meaning of life.

This has certainly been true in my own experience. Once we are aware that we are dying, life takes on a new urgency. Life takes on a new importance. When we become aware that there *is* an end to it all, we pack as much meaning as we can into the present moment. This is what this first Sunday in Advent is all about—to pack as much meaning as we can into this present time.

It is a sobering awareness, but it is not a frightful awareness. Even though we may not know what the future brings, we all are able to face the future with hope. The first candle on the Advent wreath is the candle of hope; it says to us that not only will God pack our present moment with meaning, but that the same God who was there at the beginning of all time, the beginning of our lives, will be there at the end of all time. The same God who was at the beginning is going to be at the end.

Today we worship a God of unlimited, unconditional love who is going to give us everything we need to bring us into wholeness.

We have a sober day today. We have a day that is stark in its reality of reminding us of the shortness—and the end—of life. But we also have a day that is balanced by hope, hope in knowing that God is still working with us every step of the way to have us become the people he has created us to be.

One day a little girl climbed up into the lap of her grandmother. "Read to me, Grandmama," she asked. So the grandmother took a Bible from a table beside the chair, opened it to Genesis, and began to read the creation story. As that marvelous story unfolded, the little girl became very quiet and attentive. About midway through the story, the grandmother looked at the little girl. "What do you think about that, my dear?" she asked.

"Oh, I love it because you never know what God is going to do next!"

This is the hope for us this first Sunday of Advent. We never know what God is going to do with us next. But we are to be prepared for something new because there is not one of us who does not need to have some part of our life revised, some part of our life rejuvenated, some part of our life injected with new enthusiasm.

There is a deadness in some parts of our lives which needs to be brought back to life. There is a brokenness somewhere in us that needs to be healed, and there is a fear about the future that needs to be filled with hope.

As we prepare on this first Sunday of Advent, it is time to ask ourselves, "What is it about me that needs to be brought back to life? What is it about me that needs to be changed? What is it about me that I know is not the way God would have me to live? What do I wish were different?"

We always come to New Year's Day making resolutions, don't we? We come to this New Year's Day preparing ourselves—in our souls and in our hearts—by asking God to make us new in ways that only he can do.

So Happy New Year, my friends. Yes, this is a time of soberness, but also a time for hope. Right now, the church is out of step and out of tune with the world. We will not hear Christmas music in church during this time of preparation. We need to be quieter than the world outside tells us to be. Voices outside tell us to "get busy; get ready; don't miss out; get a jump on the shopping." That seems to be the phrase this year. *Get a jump on it!*

But the world is saying a different thing to us today from the guidance the church is giving. The church tells us to turn inward for awhile…to ask some questions about ourselves…to approach this holy season with the hope that God has the power, the grace, and the will to make us into the persons he has created us to be.

Thanks be to God for his marvelous gift of hope.

Are You Ready for Christmas Yet?

MARK 1:1–8

The beginning of the good news of Jesus Christ, the son of God. As it is written in the prophet Isaiah, "See, I am sending my messenger ahead of you, who will prepare your way; the voice of one crying out in the wilderness: 'Prepare the way of the Lord, make his paths straight.'" John the Baptizer appeared in the wilderness, proclaiming a baptism of repentance for the forgiveness of sins. And people from the whole Judean countryside and all the people of Jerusalem were going out to him, and were baptized by him in the river Jordan, confessing their sins. Now John was clothed with camel's hair, with a leather belt around his waist, and he ate locusts and wild honey. He proclaimed, "The one who is more powerful than I is coming after me; I am not worthy to stoop down and untie the thong of his sandals. I have baptized you with water; but he will baptize you with the Holy Spirit."

About this time every year a bewildering question emerges in our conversations with one another. It happened to me about two weeks ago. I was at the hospital and when the elevator opened, I went inside quietly, very worried about the person I was going to see. Since I was reflecting on what that situation might be, I was barely aware of my surroundings. After a few moments of silence, the one other person on the elevator broke through my reflection with that haunting question. "Are you ready for Christmas yet?"

Immediately my mind started racing. How in the world do I respond to that question? I wondered. Was she asking me if I had put up our Christmas tree yet, or if we had mailed all of our Christmas cards, or if we had bought all the presents we have to buy? Was she even asking if we had bought our Christmas turkey?

I was saved when the elevator door opened. As I stepped out into the hall, I answered back, very lamely, "Nope, not yet!"

Are you ready for Christmas yet? I hate that question because it usually implies all the clutter that gets in our way this time of year… clutter having nothing to do with the Christ mass…and totally misses the meaning of what this time of year *should be* for us.

We hear John thundering the same question in this morning's gospel reading. In fact, that question was asked six hundred years before John when the great prophets kept asking God's chosen people, "Are you ready to receive the One whom God has promised? Are you ready to take on a whole new way of living once the Messiah comes? Are you open to a whole new way of life once you have a human example of how life is to be lived according to God's plan?"

There had been three hundred years of silence between the last of the prophets who asked these questions and John the Baptizer. The question John asked his people then—"Are you ready for Christ mass in your own life?"—is the same question he addresses to us now. "Are you ready to be open to possibilities undreamed of thus far in your life?"

John the Baptizer is one of my favorite characters in all of Holy Scripture. Why? Maybe the way he dressed. He defied convention. All of the prophets used to dress in fine clothes— much like we dress for church—but John chose to wear animal skins. He loved wild honey. I do, too. He ate bugs. I don't go that far, but it intrigues me that he did.

But it is not what he wore; it is not what he ate; it is not really how he looked. His actions and words make him such a great authority for me. He lived a life of radical simplicity. He lived totally outside of all the trappings and conventions of how he *should* look and what he *should* do. But he lived a life of radical openness to God's guidance, and he was calling all of the people of his day to that same radical openness.

John was God's bulldozer. He was God's battering ram. He was God's lightning rod. He brought truth to people in a way that stirred them to their souls, and that is why he was a radical prophet. The word "radical" always means "to get to the root of things," and John the Baptist was a radical proponent of the truth, so his expression of truth always created uneasiness in those who heard it.

So John the Baptizer is asking us today, "Are you ready for Christ mass in your life? Are you ready to become the birthplace of the Christ child anew? Are you ready to begin living your life in such a way that it somehow follows the example of that child all divine?"

Facing those questions during Advent is going to take a lot of courage—courage to enter into the spirit of this season. Advent is about change—*radical* change—which God is about to bring upon the earth; radical change not just in cosmic terms, but in intimate, personal terms as well. How much are we willing to be changed in light of what God expects of our lives?

John the Baptizer had a word that he used for this, a word which I am afraid sounds too religious. "Repentance" is the word. It is not a word which makes a whole lot of impact on us because we somehow equate the word with the super-religiosity meant for people who are devoting their whole lives to living in obedience. It is not a word that applies much to us garden-variety Christians, I'm afraid. But when John used this word he wanted each of us to take it seriously. Are there other ways we can translate repentance to make it real for us? What about "let down your guard"? Does that have any meaning? Let down your guard. Drop your defenses. Take off your mask. Face yourself honestly.

What are the values that guide your behavior? Are they the values that God shows you in the servant Christ? How do you treat those who are closest to you? When Isaiah talks about the "coming One," Isaiah isn't talking about a Messiah who has both pistols drawn and long skinny fingers of judgment pointed at us. Listen to what Isaiah says again: "*Comfort, comfort* my people, speak *tenderly* to Jerusalem." Just think about this soft image of God, the shepherd who takes us as lambs into his bosom and cradles us and comforts us tenderly. This is the kind of God who wills to be born into our lives. This is the kind of person God wills us to be. If we have a hard time loving those who are close to us, what about those who hate us? We are called to love those as well. How much of our lives are we willing to place at the disposal of God's purpose? How much more is going to be asked of us in our own servanthood, in our own willingness to give beyond ourselves? Unsettling, radical questions they are, but they all are questions which have a promise at the end.

This promise of a new life is a life of abundance; it is a life of joy; it is a life of fulfillment; it is a life of meaning. Only when we are willing to give our life away are we going to have any hope of finding it.

It takes courage, doesn't it, to drop our guard, to let down our defenses, to take off our masks, to face ourselves as we really are? Then after we've done that, we need to ask ourselves, "What does God want to be different about me?" This question is no little spiritual self-help exercise that John the Baptist is holding out. This question goes to the root of our soul.

"What is it that God wants to be different about my life?" is a demanding question that takes lots of courage to face directly. The longer I live and the more complex I know life to be, the more admiration I have for my friends who are struggling with the recovery from addiction to alcohol…as they talk with me about the first steps toward sobriety and recovery. Every one of us has an addiction of some sort that we struggle with every day. Sometimes the addiction doesn't have a name, but it is something that preoccupies us and tends to motivate us.

My alcoholic friends tell me that the first step toward healing, recovery, and wholeness lies in what they call a "fearless moral inventory." A fearless moral inventory implies courage. It takes courage for me to let down my defenses. It takes courage for me to stop pretending. It takes courage for me to drop my guard. It takes courage for me to say, "God, how do you want my life to be different from what it is?" John the Baptizer was a man of courage, and he encourages each of us to be people of courage.

Are you ready to have that kind of courage? Are you ready for Christ mass in your own life this year? Are you ready for the kind of new life it is liable to bring? Are you ready to risk what you are now for the promise of what God might bring forth?

If you are, I wish you a courageous Advent.

Stir Up Sunday

LUKE 3:7–18

John said to the crowds that came out to be baptized by him, "You brood of vipers! Who warned you to flee from the wrath to come? Bear fruits worthy of repentance. Do not begin to say to yourselves, 'We have Abraham as our ancestor'; for I tell you, God is able from these stones to raise up children to Abraham. Even now the ax is lying at the root of the trees; every tree therefore that does not bear good fruit is cut down and thrown into the fire." And the crowds asked him, "What then should we do?" In reply he said to them, "Whoever has two coats must share with anyone who has none; and whoever has food must do likewise." Even tax collectors came to be baptized, and they asked him, "Teacher, what should we do?" He said to them, "Collect no more than the amount prescribed for you." Soldiers also asked him, "And we, what should we do?" He said to them, "Do not extort money from anyone by threats or false accusation, and be satisfied with your wages." As the people were filled with expectation, and all were questioning in their hearts concerning John, whether he might be the Messiah, John answered all of them by saying, "I baptize you with water; but one who is more powerful than I is coming; I am not worthy to untie the thong of his sandals. He will baptize you with the Holy Spirit and fire. His winnowing fork is in his hand, to clear his threshing floor and to gather the wheat into his granary; but the chaff he will burn with unquenchable fire." So, with many other exhortations, he proclaimed the good news to the people.

Stir us up!

This is truly what the whole Advent season is about. It is not just a change of colors; it is not just a change in interior design with the addition of this lovely wreath and candles. This season is pointing us to a whole new way of life.

John the Baptizer came to stir people up. He came to create a whole new awareness about life. He came to make a difference. John the Baptist came to change folks, not just leave them where they are. He came demanding action. He did not want people just to be thinking lofty thoughts or having good feelings. John the Baptizer came to change: change attitudes, change habits, change perspectives, change values, and change the way people lived. These were his words then: "I have come to change you."

For John, it was a relentless quest.

Most of us resist pretty quickly when we hear somebody telling us that we must change. We put up all kinds of defenses and barriers saying, "Me change? What right do you have to ask *me* to change anything about *my* life?" John the Baptist did just that, regardless of the resistance which occurs when anybody asks us to change anything about ourselves.

But this was his purpose. It is fascinating to me that the people to whom he spoke in this instance not only heard his thunderous voice and his stern, harsh, critical, judgmental words, but that they actually stayed with him. They even asked him the all-important question about change: "What must I do? What is there about me that needs to be different?"

No change in life can occur unless we first ask this question. What is it about me that needs to be changed?

Well, here we are. This wild, weird man, John the Baptizer, demands that people take on a whole new way of being. Not only did John get the attention of these people, keep them with him, and open them up to tell them more, but his message was very simple and clear. It was not revolutionary; it was not radical. John didn't come on the scene in order to upset all the institutions of life. John came to make some very simple, clear directives to people who dared to ask the questions: "What then shall I do? What needs to be different about me?" And his words were right on target.

"What I want you to do is to possess integrity and practice compassion," John said. This is the challenge of Advent for us…to possess integrity in everything you do…to practice compassion in everything you do.

John began to spell out this message dramatically. When a big crowd gathered, they asked him first, almost as a Greek choral voice, "What should we do then, John, in order to avoid this great day of judgment that you say is coming? What should we do?"

"If you have two coats in your closet and you know somebody who has no coat, you get one of those coats and you take it to him," John said simply. It is as simple as this: When you sit down to your Sunday dinner, if you have enough to eat and you have some leftovers for Sunday evening, share what you have with someone who is not going to have anything to eat this Sunday noon.

As simple as that. To share is to repent. It is the hallmark of repentance. And unless our hearts are so softened by the needs of others and our willingness to give of ourselves in response to what we know is there, we have an unrepentant heart and life and the presence of Christ cannot dwell therein. John knew this truth about himself; he knew it about us as well.

Tax collectors were the greediest, most despicable characters on earth in John's day. These folks were in the Roman IRS. They were foreigners sent there not only to extract taxes, but they were using much of the taxes to build pagan temples. They were also skimming a lot off the top for themselves. But these tax collectors had the humility to go to John and say, "In spite of my life, I want to know what I can do differently." John was equally clear with the IRS people. "Take only what the government gives you as your salary and don't take one penny more from these people who don't even know how to read those tax forms," John said simply. "You have been living off of these people's ignorance; now is the time for you to stop. It's as simple as that."

Then soldiers came up with all their military regalia, probably with their weapons and all their mantle of armor. These were the military police in that part of the world. They were foreigners, too. They were not Jewish. They were Romans hired by the government. They were mercenaries. But these invincible people were somehow touched by John's message of repentance and confrontation. "What should we do?" they asked.

"It's simple; I want you to stop your police brutality," John said. "I want you to stop extorting. I want you to stop selling protection to these poor helpless people. I want you to stop accusing them of things they didn't do, frightening them to death and making them pay you. Be content with your wages."

A matter of justice, a matter of economics, a matter of politics, a matter of honesty, a matter of integrity, and a matter of compassion. That is what John says our life should entail. How much integrity do we have in what we do with our life day in and day out? How much does compassion form and shape our decisions and behaviors? John didn't tell them to stop doing what they were doing; he didn't tell them to get ordained or to go into a monastery. He didn't tell them to be social workers. He told them to stay right there where they belong, doing what they were doing, but to do it in an entirely different way. Do it with a whole new set of values, new standards, new ways of making decisions, and a whole new orientation on work and relationships. It is simple and clear with smashing directness.

So when John talks to us today, do we dare to open ourselves and say, "What needs to be changed about me?" Then we begin to measure ourselves against those two virtues—integrity and compassion. How do we measure up?

John is not telling us to leave what we are doing. John is telling us to be people of integrity and compassion in our own homes, in our own workplaces, on the golf course, at our cocktail parties, and in our neighborhoods. We are to be people of integrity and compassion because only in so doing can we make room in our lives for the presence of Christ which is about to come.

It is pretty simple to me; it is pretty direct, pretty individualistic. John knew that changes have to happen in the hearts of individuals before any institutions can be affected. This morning, this is where we come in, my friends.

This third Sunday of Advent is a day of joy. Is there any joy in what I have said? The message sounds pretty confronting, pretty threatening, and it makes us uneasy, doesn't it? Yes, it does to me, and I hope it does to you. But that pink candle on the Advent wreath reminds us that this is the day of joy. The Roman Catholics call that a gaudeo candle. "Gaudeo" means "to be joyful."

John had a secret. John knew something we don't know, which is what made him a good forerunner for the presence of Christ. John knew that it is only through living with integrity and compassion that we can get at life's deepest meaning and find life's greatest joy. Mystery? Yes! Simple? Yes! The third Sunday of Advent says to us, "Just do it!"

Two Things, and That's All

MATTHEW 3:1–11

In those days John the Baptist appeared in the wilderness of Judea, proclaiming, "Repent, for the kingdom of heaven has come near." This is the one of whom the prophet Isaiah spoke when he said, "The voice of one crying out in the wilderness: 'Prepare the way of the Lord, make his paths straight.'" Now John wore clothing of camel's hair with a leather belt around his waist, and his food was locusts and wild honey. Then the people of Jerusalem and all Judea were going out to him, and all the region along the Jordan, and they were baptized by him in the river Jordan, confessing their sins.

But when he saw many Pharisees and Sadducees coming for baptism, he said to them, "You brood of vipers! Who warned you to flee from the wrath to come? Bear fruit worthy of repentance. Do not presume to say to yourselves, 'We have Abraham as our ancestor'; for I tell you, God is able from these stones to raise up children to Abraham. Even now the ax is lying at the root of the trees; every tree therefore that does not bear good fruit is cut down and thrown into the fire. "I baptize you with water for repentance, but one who is more powerful than I is coming after me; I am not worthy to carry his sandals. He will baptize you with the Holy Spirit and fire."

*H*ope and *change*. They are words which really can replace those good old biblical words, "judgment" and "repentance." We get uneasy with those two words. They are off-putting; we begin to close our minds and shut down our hearts when we face judgment and repentance. It may be better to hear these words "hope" and "change" than it is to hear about judgment and repentance, but they are all interchangeable from the mouth of John bar Zachariah, John the Baptizer.

One of the most amazing things about John was that he drew the sophisticates of his time to him. He stayed out in the wilderness; he stayed on the riverbank. People came to him from their centers of learning, business, industry, wealth, and status. They flocked to him from Jerusalem and all of those inhabited areas along the river Jordan. There was something about him that spoke to the heart of those people who seemed to have everything. We in the Church of the Advent are very close to those people who have everything. So maybe as John the Baptizer spoke to the hunger of those hearts, then he can speak to the hunger of our hearts now.

Hope and change—the two words that beg for our response today. Some of you may be saying, "Oh gee, there is no way I can be any different." A lot of people say that people cannot change. If we believe Sigmund Freud, by the time we are six years old, the script has been written, and we play it out the rest of our days. "No one can change," we say. We say this about ourselves, "I'm just the way I am, and I can't be any different."

John the Baptizer didn't believe that for one minute, so he kept on proclaiming, thundering this theme of judgment, repentance, hope, and change. He knew there would be enough power in one coming after him to change even the most hardened of our hearts and the most closed of our minds. So he continued to talk about judgment and repentance.

They are really wonderful words. "Judgment" means that God actually cares about what happens to us, and that what we do really means something to God. This is what judgment means. "Repentance" means that there is something about every one of us that needs turning inside out, needs redirecting and refocusing. We need to change our minds and our hearts and our behaviors. That is what repentance means. Every one of us knows in our heart of hearts that there is a lot about us which needs to be changed.

Maybe we are demoralized; maybe we have lived with a habit, a behavior, or an attitude so long that we say, "Well, nothing can change that; why even think about it?" John the Baptizer says, "Not only think about it, but do something about it because there is power in one who can change even the most intractable of us."

Hope and change. John would not talk about judgment and repentance if he didn't believe things could be different. He says to prepare for something different, to get ready for a new way of being. *"Prepare ye the way of the Lord."*

Now how do we do that? Not by saying, "I'm going to leave the Church of the Advent today, and I'm going to be a whole new different kind of husband…" Or, "I'm going to be the best spouse there can be…" Or, "Tomorrow when I go to work, I'm going to treat everybody around me differently…" Or, "When I see those students sitting in front of me, I'm going to see them as brand new creatures."

Setting ourselves up for that kind of unrealistic expectation is going to demoralize us by Wednesday, and we will be back to where we started. When we think about change in behavior, we need to think about being specific...about taking baby steps.

The insights in a book I have been reading this Advent may help us prepare for change. It's a book called *A Year to Live*, subtitled *How to Live This Year As If It Were Your Last*. The author, Stephen Levine, has lived his life serving people on the brink of death. He lives his days mainly with people in cancer wards, on death rows, and in AIDS hospices. So he lives on the brink of the end of life all the time. Almost feeling weighed down by the heaviness of the kind of care he extended to these people, he decided to experiment with something for himself, and he invited some other people to join him in his experiment.

He found out some amazing things. When he imagined that he had maybe only one more year to live, life looked entirely different to him. He began to relate to people with more tenderness and compassion than he ever had before. He began to take people sitting next to him with more seriousness than he ever had. He began to feel a sense of compassion which had never been a part of his life. He began to feel a sense of joy and excitement in simply being given one more day.

The group of people he had invited to go through a year's imaginary journey with him also agreed to live with this reality. I have one more year to live; how am I going to live it? What's going to happen to my values, my behavior, my attitude, my way of relating to people around me? The experiment converted and revolutionized the life of everybody who engaged in it.

As I have been reading this book, I have become more and

more aware that maybe this is exactly the reason Jesus lived his life with the integrity and the depth and the power that he did. From the moment he gathered his small community around him, he began doing what? He began telling them that he was going to die soon, that he was going to be leaving them pretty quickly. They didn't want to hear those words. Like all of us, they wanted to deny the truth, but over and over he kept saying, "We don't have too long to be together, and we must make the most of the time we do have."

A year of your life—if you have only one more to live, how will you live it? This is part of preparing for the way of the Lord, and it's not a morbid way of thinking or living. John was surely God's battering ram, but he was not a spiritual depressant. He came to energize us and to challenge us and to call us into new possibilities. Somehow those new possibilities seem sharper and more engaging when we know that we don't have all the time in the world to live them out.

Hope and change. We prepare by seeing the shortness and uncertainty of human life. Then we do two other things. As you go through Advent this year, write down two hopes that you have about things that need changing in your life. Two things, and that's all. Two things. Not a brand new person, not a whole new creation. Two things that you hope can be different in your life.

Then, under those two hopes, write two things you are willing to do to make those hopes become real. Two specific intentions that you are willing to commit yourself to which will begin to make a radical change in your life.

And then, write two prayers asking God to give you what you cannot give yourself in terms of making the changes that you know you need to make. This is what repentance is all about. It means hoping for change, being willing to make a commitment to work for that, but being humble enough to say, "Oh God, there are things that I cannot change about me that I know need changing."

There is a weird word in the New Testament that comes out in English as repentance; the word is "metanoia." It is the opposite of "paranoia." Paranoia is a scattered mind, a fractured mind, a broken mind, a frantic mind. Metanoia is a single mind, a peaceful mind, a gathered mind, a focused mind. Metanoia is what John the Baptizer calls us to. Yes, it's hard work—an uneasy challenge—but it is the only way to open ourselves to the new way of life which Jesus Christ models for us all.

Pieces of Clay

Repentance and forgiveness are the two bookends of John's Gospel. Without repentance, forgiveness is impossible. With repentance, forgiveness is guaranteed and a whole new way of life can then begin. The Greek word for forgiveness means "to let go or to set free." It means that we are no longer to wallow in our guilt. The more aware we become of our sinfulness and the more fully we open that up to God, the more fully we can receive the forgiveness which God wishes to give to each one of us. "All flesh shall see the salvation of God," says John. Every one of us here today needs to repent and be receptive to the gift of God's forgiveness.

John's name in Hebrew means "God is gracious," and he spells out the grace of God by calling us to repentance. We become aware of potential we have failed to develop. We know God demands more of us than we are willing to be and therefore we repent. Advent is not for those who are complacent today, thinking we have it made, religiously, or socially, or economically. Advent is for the uneasy, the repentant. St. Thérèse of Liseux, a French nun, captures this aspect of repentance better than any I know. She says in one of her devotional writings, "If one can bear the burden of being displeasing to oneself, then one may be a very pleasant place for Jesus to reside." Wow, that's it! If one can bear the burden of being displeasing to oneself (repentance), then one may become a very pleasant place for Jesus to reside (forgiveness).

———

Advent is a season full of questions which disturb and unsettle us but prepare us for something new in the midst of our real life. How is it with your family? How open and nurturing are you with your spouse and your children? Is your family a loving, creative community, or is it lonely? Is it tense, brittle, closed, or broken? John the Baptist says to you, "*Expect* your life to be different. *Hope* for something new. It is *never* too late to change."

Christmastide

At Christmas we celebrate the formation of God's love being centered in the birth of the Holy Child. As the potter shapes and centers the lump of clay, it is made ready to be opened up and given its concrete form.

CHRISTMAS PRAYER: Gracious God, as we approach the mystery of this Holy Night, give us, we pray, the devotion of Mary, the dedication of Joseph, the joy of the angels, the adoration of the shepherds, and the curiosity of the wise men; so that we may open our minds, our hearts, our lives, to receive anew the promise of new life which you give to us again, in the birth of a tiny baby into our world. AMEN

All I Want for Christmas

LUKE 2:1–20

In those days a decree went out from Emperor Augustus that all the world should be registered. This was the first registration and was taken while Quirinius was governor of Syria. All went to their own towns to be registered. Joseph also went from the town of Nazareth in Galilee to Judea, to the city of David called Bethlehem, because he was descended from the house and family of David. He went to be registered with Mary, to whom he was engaged and who was expecting a child. While they were there, the time came for her to deliver her child. And she gave birth to her firstborn son and wrapped him in bands of cloth, and laid him in a manger, because there was no place for them in the inn. In that region there were shepherds living in the fields, keeping watch over their flock by night. Then an angel of the Lord stood before them, and the glory of the Lord shone around them, and they were terrified. But the angel said to them, "Do not be afraid; for see—I am bringing you good news of great joy for all the people: to you is born this day in the city of David a Savior, who is the Messiah, the Lord. This will be a sign for you: you will find a child wrapped in bands of cloth and lying in a manger." And suddenly there was with the angel a multitude of the heavenly host, praising God and saying, "Glory to God in the highest heaven, and on earth peace among those whom he favors!" When the angels had left them and gone into heaven, the shepherds said to one another, "Let us go now to Bethlehem and see this thing that has taken place, which the Lord has made known to us." So they went with haste and found Mary and Joseph, and the child lying in the manger. When they saw this, they made known what had been told them about this child; and all who heard it were amazed at what the shepherds told them. But Mary treasured all these words and pondered them in her heart. The shepherds returned, glorifying and praising God for all they had heard and seen, as it had been told them.

Merry Christmas!

The long wait has finally ended. All of a sudden expectations turn into an event, and hope turns into a happening. And it came to pass…long ago and far away…in the reign of Caesar Augustus…in a poor little village named Bethlehem…behind the only overcrowded hotel in the city…in a cave where farm animals ate and slept…a birth occurred. A birth of a child, a very special child, the Holy Child, and in this moment of birthing God touched the earth. God touched human life, and it has never been the same since.

And it came to pass in *those* days—and it comes to pass in *these* days—that God still wills to be born in his people anew and to touch life here in this place in such a way that it will never be the same again.

Let me give you an example of what makes this season so wondrous and so special. A five-year-old boy was riding with his mother on the last frantic trip to the mall before the stores closed for Christmas. As they were fighting their way through hectic traffic, the mother nervously said to the little child, "Bobby, you've just got to get your final list for Santa Claus; time is running out." As they drove along, he was quiet; finally he spoke. "Mama, this year I've decided that all I want for Christmas are some more hugs and kisses for my heart because it is running kind of low," he said. "Besides, I have already got enough toys anyway."

That is what makes this wondrous season so holy and so special...because God understands the wisdom of that five-year-old child. He knows that all of us hunger for more hugs and kisses for our heart because we are running kind of low. This is the reason that holy night occurred in that place long ago and far away, but also right here and now. Through the child born that night in a stable, God continues to pour out to each of us hugs and kisses for our stressed and broken hearts.

It had been a grueling last month for the young holy family. Joseph knew he had to take his bride-to-be to his hometown so they could register themselves there. He knew that she was close to delivery. So they started walking a couple of weeks before she was to deliver—walking a distance about as far as Spartanburg is from Columbia—on foot all the way...on hot, rough, and dirty roads. Perhaps those who have given birth to a child can identify with what Mary must have been feeling during that long walk. Those who have stood by their wives also know the anxiety of wanting to protect and care for and make sure everything goes right. When they got to Bethlehem, they had no reservations for lodging. It was a hurried trip; they had not made any plans, and all the rooms were taken. They received the bad news from the innkeeper and frantically wondered what in the world to do. Mary's contractions were coming closer and closer…closer and closer. Finally, in the goodness of their hearts, the innkeepers took them behind the hotel to a place where they kept their animals—a dry cave where the animals slept and ate. The innkeeper made a place for Mary there, and the young mother gave birth to her child. The innkeepers brought a receiving blanket to wrap him in and the mother gently placed him in the feeding trough with a bed of straw as his baby mattress.

On that night, God took on diapers; God was now in the skin. God had become one of us. God was at that moment entering into every aspect of life which any of us would ever know.

I don't think it was by accident that the first Christmas happened at night either. I also don't think it was by accident that the first word of this holy birth was spoken to working people— simple, ordinary working folks out doing their jobs. Because that birth occurred at that moment and the announcement was made to those people, the good news is of great joy to all of us.

No matter what kind of darkness we live in, no matter what kind of nights or nightmares we may be experiencing, God is there to hug and kiss our hurt and broken hearts. No matter what kinds of jobs we do—no matter how tedious, no matter how boring, no matter how oppressive, no matter how high-pressured they might be—God has entered into that part of life with each of us and has given us an abiding presence in whatever we do.

The child was given a special name—more than Jesus. The child was called Emmanuel, a strange name which means simply, "I want to come close to you." I want to come close to *you*. This is why the Holy Child entered life that cold night in the midst of loneliness, darkness, and homelessness...in the midst of fear and anxiety. This was no mansion, no palace, and no comfortable birthing room. This was the floor of a cave on which the Holy Child was born.

Because of that experience, there is not one of us here tonight who should feel cut off from the continuing extension of God's self to us. It is no wonder this holy season evokes such deep feelings. When God came that close, he wanted to draw from us all of the love and all of the tenderness and all of the joy that we can possibly feel. Only a baby can do that!

It is no surprise that during this time we feel an uncharacteristic sense of generosity, gratitude, sensitivity to others, and tenderness to the pain in the world. That was a crowded world then; this is a crowded world now. That was a messy world then, and this is a messy world now. Yet God still chooses to be born into the midst of the mess, and that's the good news we celebrate.

Because God has been willing...because God has made himself available to us in this way...because God has reached out and hugged and kissed our hurt and broken hearts, we can say to one another as God's people, "Merry Christmas!"

*H*earts a-Bustin' with Love

LUKE 2:1–20

In those days a decree went out from Emperor Augustus that all the world should be registered. This was the first registration and was taken while Quirinius was governor of Syria. All went to their own towns to be registered. Joseph also went from the town of Nazareth in Galilee to Judea, to the city of David called Bethlehem, because he was descended from the house and family of David. He went to be registered with Mary, to whom he was engaged and who was expecting a child. While they were there, the time came for her to deliver her child. And she gave birth to her firstborn son and wrapped him in bands of cloth, and laid him in a manger, because there was no place for them in the inn. In that region there were shepherds living in the fields, keeping watch over their flock by night. Then an angel of the Lord stood before them, and the glory of the Lord shone around them, and they were terrified. But the angel said to them, "Do not be afraid; for see—I am bringing you good news of great joy for all the people: to you is born this day in the city of David a Savior, who is the Messiah, the Lord. This will be a sign for you: you will find a child wrapped in bands of cloth and lying in a manger." And suddenly there was with the angel a multitude of the heavenly host, praising God and saying, "Glory to God in the highest heaven, and on earth peace among those whom he favors!" When the angels had left them and gone into heaven, the shepherds said to one another, "Let us go now to Bethlehem and see this thing that has taken place, which the Lord has made known to us." So they went with haste and found Mary and Joseph, and the child lying in the manger. When they saw this, they made known what had been told them about this child; and all who heard it were amazed at what the shepherds told them. But Mary treasured all these words and pondered them in her heart. The shepherds returned, glorifying and praising God for all they had heard and seen, as it had been told them.

Merry Christmas! I have pondered for weeks about how to reflect on the Christmas Gospel this year. It's a different kind of world we live in this Christmas, Christmas 2001. I don't know that the world will *ever* be safe for us again. I don't know that we will *ever* know the peace and security we knew this time last year. All of us see life as much more fragile now; all of us are aware of the power of evil that still exists in the world.

It is so easy to get caught up in the sentiment of this season and deny and neglect all of the pain that is imbedded in this life…not just pain that we share as a nation and as a world, but the changes which have happened in our own personal lives and the pain these changes bring to us. So if the Christmas Gospel is to say anything, it has to speak to the pain in the darkness. It has to be seen within the context of the world's fragility and the ever-present force of evil.

The more I've thought about this, the more I have realized that it has really never been that much different for the world, for human beings. In the Old Testament, Isaiah talks about people who walk in a land of deep darkness. He talks about the tramping boots of the warriors. He talks about blood, innocent blood, being shed regularly.

When the birth of the Christ child happened, it was not much different then either. There was terrible oppression in the Holy Land. We find it easy to forget the fact that Jesus was born to a homeless couple, born in the midst of rejection. And not too many days after his birth, the threatened ruler of the territory in which he was born sent out a decree that all of the male children who were born should be killed because he was afraid of being dethroned. The slaughter of infants. We remember that awful day. We call it Holy Innocents Day in the liturgical cycle.

Life truly never has been that different. But once again we hear the Christmas story in the midst of the darkness of our time and the pain of our living. And we hear the story as the fulfillment of the love story which began in creation. God loved this world because of its beauty, its goodness, and God's heart breaks because of its ugliness and its evil and its sorrow.

But the love story continues. It began in creation and was never snuffed out. When we celebrate this sacred time, we celebrate the culmination of a love story which did not end several millennia ago. It's a love story which continues to this very moment. I have wondered often about what makes this season so electric. I have wondered, in spite of all of the pain of life we all know so well, what it is about this holy season which gives our joy such a powerful lift. The more I have reflected on this mystery, the more I see that it boils down to one word, one powerful, dynamic, transforming, life-giving word.

The word is love. And the love story continues. As I think about my life and the lives of other people whom I know so well, only love could inspire the generosity and the gratitude and the tenderness that we feel at this time of the year. Only love has the power to bring light into darkness. Only love has the power to sustain us in our grief, to strengthen us in our times of fear and loneliness, to guide us in our wandering and confusing days. It is only love that gives life any meaning at all.

A nineteenth-century English poet captured the heart of this season. Christina Rosetti was a poet who drew most of her inspiration from her religious experience. She was influenced by the Oxford movement, which was trying to force the English church to restore the Catholic influence to that part of Christendom. Most of Rosetti's poetry is set in a sort of holy gloom. But there are a few breaks in her gloom. One of those is my favorite poem of hers, one that has been turned into a carol and set to music.

> Love came down at Christmas,
> Love all lovely, Love Divine;
> Love was born at Christmas,
> Star and angels gave the sign.
> Worship we the Godhead,
> Love Incarnate, Love Divine,
> Worship we our Jesus,
> But wherewith for sacred sign?
> Love shall be our token,
> Love be yours and Love be mine,
> Love to God and all men,
> Love for plea and gift and sign.

Love it is; love came down at Christmas. Because of that, the love story goes on…in spite of all the negativities of life that threaten to snuff it out.

One of my favorite wildflowers is called *Euonymus americanus*. It's a mountain flower; a common name for it is strawberry bush. But "strawberry bush" does not really capture the meaning of this flower. The mountain people have it right. Every time they look at this little shrub, they give it the name "hearts a-bustin' with love." A wonderful name! My favorite flower of all.

It is not much to look at in the spring; the buds are tiny. It is not a distinguished-looking plant; it's leggy. But in the fall of the year, it comes into its own. As soon as its leaves begin to drop, a very brilliant red seed pod every bit as red as poinsettias appears on the bud end of the stem. For a couple of weeks that's all you see—the red seed pod. Then all of a sudden you look again and the seed pod has burst; inside are equally brilliant orange seeds. In the midst of the dark purplish-red background those seeds are luminous. Every time I see this wildflower, I remember that there are human hearts a-bustin' with love, too…*everywhere*.

That wildflower tells the Christmas story. It ought to be our Christmas flower, it seems to me, because what God intends for us to sense at this moment is that his heart is a-bustin' with love for each of us. No matter what life does to us, God's love is inexhaustible, is durable, and it continues to connect with us.

God asks that our hearts at this time of year be busting with love as well. Busting not only with the love that he gives to us, but also with the love that he gives to us to share with one another. Because his love took a unique form in the Nativity, we celebrate God in diapers—if we really can think about it in that way. Here is the almighty, unfathomable, omnipotent God, snuggling in a bed of hay, and all of a sudden this God has skin, bones, blood, muscle, a heart, and a brain. All of a sudden this God becomes just like us. Because of that, God has now given life a new meaning. Because of that, no part of life is untouched by his love. Think about what happens when a baby or a toddler reaches out to you. Do you drop your hands or turn your back? No. When a child reaches out to you, you automatically pick it up and snuggle it to yourself and feel those little arms wrap around your neck or your shoulder. That's what God wants each of us to experience.

The broken body of that baby is continually poured out to us in the body and the blood of the Eucharist, and the love story goes on. The manger this day is our hearts. Our hearts are where that love is to be born anew.

Yes, love came down at Christmas. Love be yours, and love be mine. Merry Christmas!

*T*insel on the Tree

MATTHEW 2:13–15, 19–23

Now after they had left, an angel of the Lord appeared to Joseph in a dream and said, "Get up, take the child and his mother, and flee to Egypt, and remain there until I tell you; for Herod is about to search for the child, to destroy him." Then Joseph got up, took the child and his mother by night, and went to Egypt, and remained there until the death of Herod. This was to fulfill what had been spoken by the Lord through the prophet, "Out of Egypt I have called my son."

When Herod died, an angel of the Lord suddenly appeared in a dream to Joseph in Egypt and said, "Get up, take the child and his mother, and go to the land of Israel, for those who were seeking the child's life are dead." Then Joseph got up, took the child and his mother, and went to the land of Israel. But when he heard that Archelaus was ruling over Judea in place of his father Herod, he was afraid to go there. And after being warned in a dream, he went away to the district of Galilee. There he made his home in a town called Nazareth, so that what had been spoken through the prophets might be fulfilled, "He will be called a Nazarene."

*I*n spite of the torrential rain outside, today is a beautiful day inside this building. The Gospel for today, however, which has been appointed for this wondrous day of baptism, is an ominous story about a threatening incident which occurred shortly after Jesus' birth. The story begins after the wise men had returned to their homelands as transformed people. In this Gospel, Joseph has a dream in which he is warned about Herod's jealousy and directed to take his family to Egypt. Once in Egypt, Joseph has another dream telling him to move his family to Israel. Mary not only has had to deliver her child in strange surroundings, but the family has been uprooted twice in the first few months of the Holy Child's life.

So the Christmas story is not set in a context of joy, peace, and security. It is set in the unfamiliar, the uncertain, the insecure, and the violent. As we hear in this story today, Jesus' life is in danger because the jealous king has decreed the killing of all newborn infant males. Jesus is born to a homeless family and his life is being threatened. Joseph's first response is to make sure that Jesus is kept safe, so they flee to a less-threatening land. This is not a pretty story, but it is fitting for this glorious day of baptism to demonstrate the constancy of God's care. Only Matthew tells the story of the flight into Egypt, in which he reminds us that life will always be uncertain, even for the Christ child. So we don't come into the Christian family expecting every day to be sunny. There will be stormy days and dark, cold nights when we have lost our direction. There will be threats to our safety and peace.

Christian faith is not an entrance into a land of paradise. Those babies nestled in your arms right now know nothing of the threatening cold and darkness. The important thing for your children is that, even though they are unaware of it, God is going to make them a promise of his presence which nothing in life can destroy. This is their birthday in a new family. God's promise will be one that will last forever.

On most birthdays, the gifts and toys will be lost or broken before sundown. But that is not the way it is with God's precious gift to these children today. The gift of God's love will go with them wherever they are for the rest of their lives, no matter what life does to them. We can't protect them from all the uncertainties about life, but we can be assured God will be with them, no matter what happens.

Inspired by this Gospel reading, a wonderful legend began in the early church which tells the story of the holy family's evasion of Herod's soldiers during the trip to Egypt. The family had to be very careful to keep from being discovered. One night the family entered the cold darkness of a cave, where they soon fell asleep, exhausted from the day's travels. A little spider, enchanted by the presence of the Christ, wanted to do something special for the child, so it began to spin a beautiful web which completely covered the entrance to the cave. A hard frost covered the web that night, sealing the entrance to the cave, keeping the family warm inside. Later that night as Herod's soldiers came by with their lanterns, the lead soldier noticed the unbroken web covering the entrance of the cave and assumed the web would be broken if anyone had entered the cave. So the soldiers marched on, leaving the holy family safe for the night.

We are not sure this story is true, but it is the reason we hang tinsel on our Christmas trees, to remind us of the frost-covered spider web that protected the Christ child. This legend is a wonderful way for us to tell a story of God's protection of us throughout our lives. This Gospel story tells us that God is aware of what is happening to us all the time, regardless of life's circumstances. It is God's continual watchfulness and intervention which we celebrate today in this sacrament of Holy Baptism. God will watch over your children from this time forward, and there will never be a moment when they will be disconnected from God's love. God is not only watching over us; God is there with us. God warns Joseph in a dream, sending messages and words of encouragement and direction. God does that for each of us all the time, through warnings and cautions and suggestions other people make. God sends messengers to us to guide us and keep us from heading into danger. This Gospel finally tells us that God will restore us when things don't go well. These children will experience pain and sorrow; we all know that. God's constant presence will be there to pick them up and return them to their special place as God's children forever.

We have many gifts given to us this day. God's presence is the one which will never fail us. This is the gift we celebrate for your children today. We welcome these children into Christ's family so we may help you remind them of that gift in the hope that the rest of their lives will be lived according to this beginning. Amen.

Practicing God's Goodness

LUKE 2:41–52

Now every year his parents went to Jerusalem for the festival of the Passover. And when he was twelve years old, they went up as usual for the festival. When the festival was ended and they started to return, the boy Jesus stayed behind in Jerusalem, but his parents did not know it. Assuming that he was in the group of travelers, they went a day's journey. Then they started to look for him among their relatives and friends. When they did not find him, they returned to Jerusalem to search for him. After three days they found him in the temple, sitting among the teachers, listening to them and asking them questions. And all who heard him were amazed at his understanding and his answers. When his parents saw him they were astonished; and his mother said to him, "Child, why have you treated us like this? Look, your father and I have been searching for you in great anxiety." He said to them, "Why were you searching for me? Did you not know that I must be in my Father's house?" But they did not understand what he said to them. Then he went down with them and came to Nazareth, and was obedient to them. His mother treasured all these things in her heart. And Jesus increased in wisdom and in years, and in divine and human favor.

Happy New Year! We have taken another step into our future in this pilgrimage we call life, and as we begin this new pilgrimage together out of the old and into the new, we have a Gospel story today about a pilgrimage. As I understand pilgrimages, they always have several levels of meaning. This is a pilgrimage, to be sure, from one place to another in terms of geography and miles, but it is also a pilgrimage in terms of a deepening and a broadening of understanding, and it is a pilgrimage as time passes and we move on into our future together.

Pilgrimage. This wonderful story is the only one we have about Jesus' childhood and only Luke remembers and records it for our memory. The Gospels do not tell us anything about what happened to Jesus in those first twelve years of his life. We know that he was born and we leave him there in the manger. Then all of a sudden he appears again at twelve in his own hometown of Nazareth where he has grown up, and when we meet him now he has begun a pilgrimage to the Holy City, Jerusalem.

It is a wonderful human interest story Luke records for us. It must have meant a lot to Luke for him to remember it and to bother to write it down. Luke must have had in mind that we too might benefit from this incident in our Lord's life as we continue on in our own pilgrimage of life for ourselves. So what is going on here? Jesus has been living in Nazareth, which is a tiny village off the main highway in Galilee. It is not a commercial hub or educational site or medical center. It has nothing really to commend it as a destination point. It is a simple, quiet, tiny place to live. Nazareth. I would imagine it is quite like Cowpens; it's a wonderful, picturesque place but is not really the center of a lot of cultural or religious activity. Yet that is where Jesus lived this first twelve years of his life. He never left. All of a sudden here he is, right on the verge of his adulthood, going to the "big city." He is going there at the time of celebration of the greatest festival of all.

I don't know if you have been to New Orleans or Mobile for a Mardi Gras, but if you have been there you have caught something of the spirit that permeated Jerusalem at this time of year. The Holy City was bustling with noisy crowds. It was crowded because every Jewish male who lived within fifteen miles of the Holy City was required to go to Jerusalem every year for Passover. Furthermore, all Jewish men, regardless of where they lived, were required to go to Jerusalem at least once in their life and gradually the women were invited to come along as well. So here we have it, the holy family on their way to the Holy City. When they got there we can imagine that Jesus was impressed by everything he saw.

He had never seen such commotion. He had heard of the temple. He had gone to his own little synagogue week in and week out. He had learned the lore of his faith. He had always heard about the Holy of Holies and the elaborate rituals and the priests, but he had never been there, and now here he was, right in the middle of it all, and he doesn't want to go home. So he decides to stay. This is where the plot thickens, especially for those of us who have raised adolescents and have known what it is to go through the ordeal of watching our children reach an age where they want to take risks and make decisions on their own without their parents' advice or approval.

An Arabic proverb says there are only two gifts we can give our children: roots and wings. It is easy to give the roots; it is hard to give the wings. But here he is, making a unilateral decision to stay behind in the Holy City while his parents start on their way back to Nazareth. As was the custom in that time, the women left first and the men stayed behind a little later and caught up with the women around a campfire that night. And so when Mary and Joseph got together around the campfire that night they said, "Where's Jesus?" "He's not with you?" "No, I thought he was with you."

Once they decided that neither of them had been with him all day they felt assured that some of their neighbors from Nazareth who were traveling with them would know where he was. In that day and time it really did take a village to raise a child and everybody knew everybody else in that small town. So the anxious parents felt hopeful that, as they went around the campfire, they would find Jesus playing with some of his buddies. When they saw he was nowhere to be found, they panicked.

If you have ever lost a child in a store or at a fair or ball game, you know what must have seized these young parents at that moment. They couldn't find him anywhere. So they hurried back to Jerusalem and for three days they looked for him. I can't imagine what that must have been like. So they started to backtrack to the Holy City, which was still crowded because the festival lasted seven days. When they went to the temple, they saw Jesus sitting in the midst of the priests.

It was the priests' responsibility during this feast to talk with pilgrims about religious questions they had. Jesus experienced a startling insight at this point in his own internal pilgrimage. He received a clear understanding of his special mission in life as the Son of God. Consequently, he wanted to stay in the temple and absorb as much wisdom and inspiration from the priests as he could. But when his parents found him, Mary, a typical concerned mother, probably yanked the boy up from where he was sitting.

I'm sure the interaction was much more intense than it sounds in scripture, because his parents were very upset. So Mary stood toe-to-toe with him and said, "Son, where in the world have you been? We have been worried sick! We have not known where you were for three days now!" Jesus gave the typical adolescent response: "Mom, you should know I'm all right; I have been in my Father's house doing my Father's business with all these nice folks. Why have you been worried about me?" I am sure the dialogue continued for a while, but Luke tells us that at the end of the conversation Jesus went back to Nazareth and spent another eighteen years in his tiny village deepening his understanding of his forthcoming mission and ministry. During this time he was learning to discover the divine in the ordinary.

You would have expected Jesus to go into a monastery after his experience in the temple, wouldn't you? Or certainly to put himself in some kind of educational environment in which he could begin to hone his skills as a priest or a rabbi. Instead, he went back home and probably took over the family business because we know his father died when he was very young. So Jesus had to run the family carpentry business for eighteen years. As he fulfilled this responsibility he learned about the presence of God in his daily life and found the divine within the mundane. He found that he was growing in his relationship with God right there at home. He didn't need to be somewhere else. And he was growing in his relationships with people in the neighborhood, people who hired him to do repairs and construction. He was finding the presence of God in the midst of the ordinary.

I think this is what Luke wants us to know. We don't need to search for the presence of the Christ in the high holy places. We find the presence of the Christ most clearly in the ordinary events of our daily lives. Our faith should make some difference as we grow in favor with God and other people. Our faith should influence how we live our daily lives. In fact, someone said one time that the test of our religious faith should be how it affects our dogs or our cats. Irenaeus was one of the early church fathers who, during the second century, said in trying to explain the incarnation, "He became as we are so that we might become like he is."

Now think about this for yourself. He became as you are so that you might become as he is. Jesus demonstrated what it was to be the Son of God as he practiced goodness every day of his life…in his own family, in his workplace, in his neighborhood, in his own little village. This is the example he leaves with us. If we do expect to find the divine presence in life and to grow in favor with God and other human beings, then we are called to practice goodness in everything we do, with every person we encounter, in every place we go. That's our *charter* for our pilgrimage in this life.

*P*ieces of Clay

And so, on this holy night, as we hear again this wonderful story, let's not try to figure it out; let's simply adore it. Let's not try to analyze it away; let's simply adore it. Let's not try to explain it to one another; let's simply adore it for what it is. Emmanuel, God's gift to be close to us, in the form of a baby.

—

Most of us know what it is to have a baby nestled into this sweet spot between our shoulder and our cheek. And when that baby is there all is well with the world. That is what Emmanuel means. It sounds like a very high theological doctrine. What it means is that God wills this holy life to snuggle into your life. Emmanuel means I want to go home and make a place for me with you. I want to draw close. I want to stoop down and be as near to you as that baby's breath is on your cheek. That's the gift! That's the wonder! That's the God who takes human form and who dares to say to each of us again as we hear this Christmas story anew, "I want to go home with you."

—

God has entered into the very heart of life to give us a deep sense that he is with us, no matter where we are. "Emmanuel" is another name for God, another name for Jesus. It is a strange word; we don't use it much. But the word means simply, "I want to come close to you." This is what this Holy Child says to each of us, because when God enters life in the form of a helpless infant, God intends to draw from us all of the tenderness, all of the love, and all of the joy that we can possibly feel as human beings. And only a baby can affect us in this way.

—

This Christmas Eve is filled with such wondrous mystery for me, because in the beginning, when it was all designed by God at least two thousand years ago, God had you and me in mind when he planned this occasion. Tonight we make the preposterous claim together that expectation all of a sudden becomes event, and hope suddenly happens, and a birth occurs, and God touches life in such a way that it will never be the same again.

I pray that a hush of grace may descend upon your souls. It is now time for us to reach another level of awareness, an awareness of the promise that as Christ was born two thousand years ago, this Christmas 2000, he still wills to be born in our hearts and our minds this very evening.

*E*piphany

During the season of Epiphany we begin to envision how this divine love made concrete will be shaped and expressed in the world, just as the potter has a vision of what the opened lump of clay will become in its completed form.

*P*RAYER FOR EPIPHANY: Gracious God, you created us out of love, you redeemed us by your love, and you sustain us with your love. Let the glory of your love be seen in each of us that we may reflect your presence and show forth your love in the world, through Jesus Christ who came to show us the way. AMEN

When the Wine Runs Out

JOHN 2:1–11

On the third day there was a wedding in Cana of Galilee, and the mother of Jesus was there. Jesus and his disciples had also been invited to the wedding. When the wine gave out, the mother of Jesus said to him, "They have no wine." And Jesus said to her, "Woman, what concern is that to you and to me? My hour has not yet come." His mother said to the servants, "Do whatever he tells you." Now standing there were six stone water jars for the Jewish rites of purification, each holding twenty or thirty gallons. Jesus said to them, "Fill the jars with water." And they filled them up to the brim. He said to them, "Now draw some out and take it to the chief steward." So they took it. When the steward tasted the water that had become wine and did not know where it came from (though the servants who had drawn the water knew), the steward called the bridegroom and said to him, "Everyone serves the good wine first, and then the inferior wine after the guests have become drunk. But you have kept the good wine until now." Jesus did this, the first of his signs, in Cana of Galilee, and revealed his glory; and his disciples believed in him.

*T*hings are not always the way they seem. That's a truth about life. This is especially true in this particular Gospel from John, who always challenges us to look below the surface for the truth hidden in the depths. John showed a talent in his writing to intrigue us with the stories themselves as he beckons us to look deep inside the story to discover important meaning for ourselves. Today's Gospel, known simply as the Wedding Feast in Cana, is one of the best examples of John's skill as a storyteller. Most of us know this story by heart. On the surface, it is a simple story about a wedding, but underneath lies a complicated incident. In forty-two years of helping people get married, I have discovered that weddings are the single most anxiety-producing experiences in life. Regardless of our most fervent wishes, a wedding is never an occasion filled with absolute, unadulterated joy.

This Gospel begins in the middle of the wedding tension. Unlike today's wedding celebrations, which involve up to twenty-four hours of intense interaction, a wedding in John's time lasted from seven to fourteen days. Guests would arrive in waves throughout the entire fortnight. In this Gospel story, Jesus entered the wedding party about midway through its course. Jesus arrived as an invited guest, but he brought with him five wedding crashers, his first five disciples. The arrival of unexpected guests can upset party hostesses; however, the problems had begun before Jesus arrived with his retinue. As Jesus stepped through the doors Mary ran up to him to tell him that they had run out of wine.

In the Eastern world in those days, being a hostess was a sacred duty which required absolute precision. It was a serious *faux pas* to run out of wine at a party, and Mary was looking to Jesus for his assistance. Not only were the wine cellars and the wine stores empty, the next batch of wine was still ripening as grapes on the vines. From Mary's reaction, we get a sense that she was the caterer or the organizer of this event. Suddenly she found no more wine to serve the guests, with many more days of the wedding celebration ahead. Mary shared her panic with Jesus, who assured her that there was no reason for alarm. Jesus instructed a few of the waiters to take the six empty water jars from the hallway and fill them to the brim with fresh water, which they did. After a few moments passed, Jesus told them to take a cupful from one of the jars and take it to the head waiter for tasting. The head waiter was amazed at the transformation. Normally at parties, the better wine is served first, followed by the lesser wines once the guests' taste buds begin to dull. At this wedding feast in Cana, however, the best wine was served throughout the latter half of the party, and the wedding celebration continued without incident. None of the guests knew that this miracle had occurred.

This is not a dramatic miracle. Our marriage service calls it "the miracle at a wedding in Cana of Galilee," but it is the quietest of all miracles. This story is not about Jesus restoring sight to a blind man or curing leprosy or returning life to the dead. In this story John tells us of the first public event in Jesus' life. This story shows how Jesus acts in such a quiet way. Cana was a tiny village, and this wedding was taking place in a small home in this rather insignificant town. John tells the story with such reserve that we need to look beneath the surface to realize the true transformation which occurred at that wedding. It doesn't really matter to John about water and wine; likewise, it shouldn't matter to us. What matters is the transformation that occurs when Jesus is present. Those six jars of water held a total of 150 to 180 gallons of wine, but John is not concerned with the specifics of the volume. Instead, John wants to show us that God's grace flows in superabundance; it is inexhaustible and freely given to any who need to receive it. The wine had run out, but with God's help there was more than enough of the best wine for everyone.

When has the wine run out of your life, and taken with it all the joy? In Jewish culture, wine and joy are inseparable; they are one and the same. When has all the joy run out? When did you run out of peace? When did the love dry up? When has hope wilted from thirst? These are the questions that John wants us to ask about this story. When has the wine run out of our living? Maybe when a job didn't turn out the way you thought it would. Maybe when you were betrayed by a person you trusted. Maybe when your health failed. Maybe when you failed at something you had struggled with for years. For all of us the wine has run out before, but there is good news. Once Jesus enters, the wine begins to flow in ways that we cannot imagine.

Mary went to Jesus with the expectation and hope that he could do something to save the wedding. Jesus did as he was asked, but it took her expressed need and hopefulness to create the miracle that occurred so quietly and powerfully. The same can happen for us when our wine runs out, and we too can experience the transformation in our lives if we express our need and maintain our hope.

You will notice that Jesus didn't do the miracle by himself; he called upon the waiters to help him gather what was needed. Jesus calls us into sharing his work of transformation. We must remember that the church has as its primary responsibility the transformation of the world around us. Today it seems the church has lost its mission given by our Lord: the mission to transform discrimination, bigotry, and segregation into a sense of beloved community. Each of us is called into that mission to transform life around us so we can conquer the evils which prevent people from being appreciated and valued as they ought to be.

Whenever Jesus enters a new scene, new wine flows. Jesus can take a joyless life, dry with self-absorption, and turn it into a life filled with wine, overflowing with joy and generosity and compassion. That is our Lord's quiet power of transformation. Today he brings new wine. Come and drink.

*H*ealers in a Hate-Torn World

MARK 2:1–12

When Jesus returned to Capernaum after some days, it was reported that he was at home. So many gathered around that there was no longer room for them, not even in front of the door; and he was speaking the word to them. Then some people came, bringing to him a paralyzed man, carried by four of them. And when they could not bring him to Jesus because of the crowd, they removed the roof above him; and after having dug through it, they let down the mat on which the paralytic lay. When Jesus saw their faith, he said to the paralytic, "Son, your sins are forgiven." Now some of the scribes were sitting there, questioning in their hearts, "Why does this fellow speak in this way? It is blasphemy! Who can forgive sins but God alone?" At once Jesus perceived in his spirit that they were discussing these questions among themselves; and he said to them, "Why do you raise such questions in your hearts? Which is easier, to say to the paralytic, 'Your sins are forgiven,' or to say, 'Stand up and take your mat and walk'? But so that you may know that the Son of Man has authority on earth to forgive sins"—he said to the paralytic—"I say to you, stand up, take your mat and go to your home." And he stood up, and immediately took the mat and went out before all of them; so that they were all amazed and glorified God, saying, "We have never seen anything like this!"

During the time of Jesus, affliction and illness were considered to be the result of sin. Hence the act of healing was seen as a sign of divine forgiveness. Such was the mindset of the people found in this Gospel. Our Lord's ministry was surrounded by suffering and disease, alienation, and brokenness of spirit. Jesus was surrounded by the pain of human beings, and he was seen in the midst of it all as a healer. In this season of Epiphany, we walk with our Lord on a road to discovery. This is a time of unveiling, new awareness, new insight, fresh revelation.

In the Gospel for today, Jesus unveils a key aspect of his ministry. In this incident Jesus is dealing with his own identity and his clarification of his mission. He identifies himself as a healer in the midst of all levels of pain. His ministry, then, is going to be defined by pain and healing for the rest of his days. This experience occurs early in Jesus' ministry in a little seaside village called Capernaum, where Jesus would eventually establish the headquarters for his ministry. People gradually discovered the house where Jesus was staying, and word spread quickly that Jesus would be there the following day. The news traveled so fast that before sunrise, the house was filled with people. The crowd had spilled onto the porch and into the streets. The gathering crowd, eager to meet Jesus, who would stand in the midst of their pain, stopped traffic.

As Jesus stood in his living room, trying to be sensitive and responsive to the people who had come to see him, four men carried their friend on a stretcher to see Jesus. When the four men crested the hill, they were dismayed at the size of the crowd. They had traveled a very long way to bring their paralyzed friend for Jesus' healing touch. They had heard of Jesus' miracles, and they had high expectations for their friend's recovery. Not to be deterred by the mob, the men carried their friend around to the back of the house, up an exterior staircase to the rooftop patio. They could not hear through the roof, so they opened up a hole in the clay-covered thatch roof and lowered their friend inside the house at the feet of Jesus.

I can imagine Jesus' smile at the ingenuity and persistence of those four friends as they lowered the stretcher safely to the ground. Jesus forgot the crowd for the moment and turned his attention to the pain of the paralyzed young man, seeing in him something nobody else saw. Whereas everyone else saw a crippled body, Jesus saw a crippled spirit. Since there was thought to be a direct relation between sickness, suffering, and sin, illness automatically indicated God's disfavor. So Jesus looked into the soul of the young man and saw that the crippled man needed a treatment called forgiveness.

We may think it archaic or even barbaric to equate sickness with sin and punishment from God, and I am glad we have grown beyond this immature understanding of tragedy and illness. We now understand the powerful psychosomatic effect of feelings on our minds and bodies. Guilt can become a physical crippler. And if guilt does not cripple our bodies, it can cripple our spirits, because unresolved guilt is one of the major causes of depression. Guilt also inhibits the body's restorative powers after injury or illness. Guilt can suppress our immune systems so that we cannot fend off diseases efficiently. Jesus knew what we know now, that unresolved guilt can have a sickening, crippling effect on our lives.

As Jesus looked into the soul of that young man, he did not tell him to get up and go home. He said, "Child, your sins have been put away." I prefer that translation to, "Son, your sins are forgiven." To me, that sounds too antiseptic. Jesus said, "Child, your sins have been put away. You do not need to worry about them anymore."

Those of us who are crippled by guilt need to hear this message from our Lord. "Child, God is not angry with you. Do not be afraid." Jesus is healing. Once we receive his healing we are given a mission in life. We are given a ministry to turn our healed pain into a new life for other people. We are placed in this life to be healers and bearers of his message wherever there is a sense of alienation or despair or crippling guilt. We are to be healers as we stand in the midst of a hate-torn world. We are not to be hate mongers; we are called to be people who wage peace. We are called to be wherever we can be signs of good news and new life.

Jesus said, "Roll up that stretcher, child, and get yourself out of here. You have a new way of life in front of you now." This is possible for all of us. It is your Lord's promise to you; receive it as it was spoken. "Child, God is not angry with you." He says, "Go on home. Do not be afraid. Roll up your stretcher and go."

Inside Out

LUKE 6:17–26

He came down with them and stood on a level place, with a great crowd of his disciples and a great multitude of people from all Judea, Jerusalem, and the coast of Tyre and Sidon. They had come to hear him and to be healed of their diseases; and those who were troubled with unclean spirits were cured. And all in the crowd were trying to touch him, for power came out from him and he healed all of them. Then he looked up at his disciples and said: "Blessed are you who are poor, for yours is the kingdom of God. Blessed are you who are hungry now, for you will be filled. Blessed are you who weep now, for you will laugh. Blessed are you when people hate you, and when they exclude you, revile you, and defame you on account of the Son of Man. Rejoice in that day and leap for joy, for surely your reward is great in heaven; for that is what their ancestors did to the prophets. But woe to you who are rich, for you have received your consolation. Woe to you who are full now, for you will be hungry. Woe to you who are laughing now, for you will mourn and weep. Woe to you when all speak well of you, for that is what their ancestors did to the false prophets."

Luke's Gospel turns us upside down to change the way we look at life. In fact, this Gospel reaches into us to turn us inside out. Luke presents us with some harsh words, presented to us as a hard-to-swallow medicine for our soul.

Luke's telling of the Beatitudes is slightly different from Matthew's version. Whereas Matthew depicts Jesus speaking from a mountaintop to the people below, Luke tells us that Jesus came down to speak to his people on the same level, shoulder to shoulder, and eye to eye. Jesus came to deliver the truth, not only as God's messenger, but also as one human being to another. Luke tells us that a throng of thousands came to see Jesus, to hear him, to be healed of their diseases, and to have their unclean spirits washed away. These people longed to hear Jesus' words and hungered for his healing. It is the same for us today. Millions of people desperately seek guidance in this life. In bookstores and libraries, shelves are packed with self-help books with titles that promise happiness and fulfillment, health and wellness, spiritual peace, and personal salvation. We look to gurus for instructions on ways to cope with stress and avoid aging. We still seek guidance. We still need to hear someone tell us how to live. We still long for healing from our human condition.

The people in this Gospel knew Jesus had the compassionate power to heal their disease, to ease their unclean spirits. We may think that unclean spirits were a biblical phenomenon, but they are a contemporary malady as well. The names may be different today, but the unclean spirits continue to affect our minds and afflict our hearts. Prejudice, arrogance, rage, violence, distrust, cynicism, and suspicion are a few of the unclean spirits which move among us and through us all the time. We don't refer to them as unclean spirits anymore; consequently, we cannot be cleansed of them because we do not properly identify them. You will notice that the sick and needy sought Jesus to be healed and cleansed. Luke tells us that Jesus healed everyone who came to see him. Each one of us brings a need for guidance, healing, and cleansing to this level place, where we all stand shoulder to shoulder and eye to eye. Jesus wants to give us the same power he gave the people then, so that our lives may have direction and hope and strength.

Sometimes we relegate our Lord to an admirable memory, a person who did great deeds a long time ago. The church today needs us to see our Lord as a living, contemporary reality who continues to do great things for all of us who seek him. He healed them all. What a promise! What an expectation! And after he healed them, he began to teach them. It is at this point that Luke turns us upside down by telling us how blessed and fortunate are the poor, the hungry, the sad and disconsolate, the hated, the scorned, and the marginalized. Would any of us choose those positions in life in order to be blessed? Jesus continues, "Woe to you who are rich and whose stomachs do not growl with hunger, those of you who are happy all the time, those of you who are popular and liked by everyone and are successful. Woe to you."

Our culture, on the other hand, promises that the blessed are the rich, the satisfied, the contented, the secure, the well accepted, and the popular, but Jesus tells us the opposite is true. What a warning that is to us! We are the rich of the world. It is a safe bet that each of us spends more on automobile expenses each month than the average Third World family spends on food for an entire year. We are rich. As uncomfortable as the message makes us feel, Jesus is talking to us.

Now I think it is important to see at the outset here that Jesus is not talking about blessing one group and cursing another, or about exalting one group and condemning another, or about judging one group as better than another. Jesus is simply saying that God's heart of compassion goes out to those who have little of what this world gives, and he cautions those who have much. We are the rich, woe to us. Jesus is not angry with us; he doesn't condemn us because we are wealthy. In fact, Jesus chose Matthew, a very rich accountant and tax collector, as one of his twelve disciples. Jesus does not condemn us because we are rich; he warns us because we are rich. Woe to you; beware if you are rich, because there is a possibility of an insidious spiritual illness that wealth can bring.

The new diagnostic term for this wealth-borne illness is "affluenza." Affluenza may cause a sense of entitlement, a subtle sense of self-reliance and self-dependency, self-absorption, and self-importance. The Lord is warning us about this illness because affluenza may infect our spirits and cause us to lose our sensitivity to those who are poor and in need. We lose our sensitivity to those who might get one meal a day. We lose our sensitivity to those people who are marginalized in our society, who are scorned and hated because they have so few of the gifts of the world. Jesus said to us, "Beware, your heart is in danger and you are in spiritual peril of losing the wholeness I want to give to you."

I know in my own life that affluenza can dim the recognition of my dependence on God and dull my gratitude to him for those gifts I have received. Affluenza also brings with it a certain anxiety about taking care of the things that we have acquired. The things we possess begin to possess us. This is part of the spiritual disease which infects our spirits. My hunger for the meaningful things in life is sometimes sated by the creature comforts I enjoy. I do not weep enough for the pain of the world when I am insulated in my environment of fulfillment. I do not recognize the need for affirmation of the humanity that exists in the darkened corners of our world when I am concerned with my own popularity. These are the symptoms of affluenza.

Jesus doesn't want us to be sick; he wants us to be whole creatures. He doesn't condemn us because we are rich, but he wants to make sure we don't lose our soul in the process. There is an ancient Hasidic saying: "It is easy for the poor to depend on God because they have nothing else to depend on; but it is hard for the rich to depend on God because their possessions are always crying out to them, 'Depend on us.'" What a subtle, insidious cancer of the soul that is. If you are discomforted by the Lord's Beatitudes, you are ready to be cleansed, healed, and freed from the shackles which wealth can bring. Open your hearts to the needs of others who are less fortunate. Give freely that which you so lavishly have been given. Experience the joy which comes from the freedom of dispossession. The warning and the promise of the Gospel. Let those who have ears to hear, hear them both.

Something Old, Something New

LUKE 2:22–40

When the time came for their purification according to the law of Moses, they brought Jesus up to Jerusalem to present him to the Lord (as it is written in the law of the Lord, "Every firstborn male shall be designated as holy to the Lord"), and they offered a sacrifice according to what is stated in the law of the Lord, "a pair of turtledoves or two young pigeons." Now there was a man in Jerusalem whose name was Simeon; this man was righteous and devout, looking forward to the consolation of Israel, and the Holy Spirit rested on him. It had been revealed to him by the Holy Spirit that he would not see death before he had seen the Lord's Messiah. Guided by the Spirit, Simeon came into the temple; and when the parents brought in the child Jesus, to do for him what was customary under the law, Simeon took him in his arms and praised God, saying, "Master, now you are dismissing your servant in peace, according to your word; for my eyes have seen your salvation, which you have prepared in the presence of all peoples; a light for revelation to the Gentiles and for glory to your people Israel." And the child's father and mother were amazed at what was being said about him. Then Simeon blessed them and said to his mother Mary, "This child is destined for the falling and the rising of many in Israel, and to be a sign that will be opposed so that the inner thoughts of many will be revealed—and a sword will pierce your own soul too." There was also a prophet, Anna the daughter of Phanuel, of the tribe of Asher. She was of a great age, having lived with her husband seven years after her marriage, and then as a widow to the age of eighty-four. She never left the temple but worshiped there with fasting and prayer night and day. At that moment she came, and began to praise God and to speak about the child to all who were looking for the redemption of Jerusalem. When they had finished everything required by the law of the Lord, they returned to Galilee, to their own town of Nazareth. The child grew and became strong, filled with wisdom; and the favor of God was upon him.

*S*ome of the rich treasures in Holy Scripture come in the form of obscure, minor characters who are impacted by Jesus' life. Nowhere is this truer than in the story of the presentation of Jesus in the temple. Today we celebrate this special occasion in the life of the holy family and a special occasion in the life of the church. Jewish custom required that children be presented to the temple priest at around six weeks of age. Forty days had to pass before a newborn baby was brought in to the temple for blessing and dedication. At the presentation, the parents would turn over the child to the priest, who held the child up and dedicated the child to God. The parents had to pay a sacrifice in order to receive the child back into their care.

In this story, six-week-old Jesus is simply lying there, far too young to speak. The two obscure characters, Simeon and

Anna, who predict his influence on the world, are heroes of the faith in this Epiphany event. Why is that? They appeal to me so much because they are very old, yet they continue to set a good example by worshipping God in the temple day after day.

Luke is the only one who tells us anything about Simeon, a man who is very old and nearing death. But Simeon is there in the temple that day with hope. Luke tells us that Simeon was looking forward, which is why Simeon appeals to me so much. How many of us in our old age look forward in hope? Most of us begin to sink at a point in life when we feel there is very little to anticipate. Here is this old prophet, looking forward with open eyes and expectant spirit. Simeon is following the Jewish tradition, waiting in the temple for the appearance of the Messiah. His preconception causes him to expect the Messiah to be a charismatic political leader or military genius. As Simeon's imagination sharpens, he sees the hope of the world, the consolation of Israel, and a new way of being for all people in the form of a helpless, vulnerable baby.

Simeon wrote, on that great occasion of joy, an exultant expression that the church has received as his legacy, known by those of us who sing Morning Prayer as the "Nunc Dimittus." This beautiful canticle is given to us by this very obscure old man. It is a poignant scene, that old man with gnarled hands, near the end of his life, taking that baby into his care. Simeon takes the Holy Child with the full assurance that a whole new way of being is coming to pass. Old Simeon, through his dim eyes, can see something that no one else in that crowded temple can see that day. He puts his walking stick up against one of those great pillars of the temple, steps out of the crowd, blesses the holy family, sings his wonderful song of departure, and disappears into the shadows of the temple, never to be heard from again.

Then appears Anna, who is even older than Simeon. No one knows her exact age, although she may be over a hundred years old. This wonderful prophetess, who has spent her entire life seeking the same thing as Simeon, walks up to the holy family, takes the child from Mary, shows him to the people in the courtyard, and tells them, "This is the One we have been expecting. This is our hope, our dream come true." Simeon and Anna, heroes of the faith, envisioned a world that never was. They recognized a new way of life that they had been longing to live. They saw God touch life with an innocent child, and their eyes were opened to new possibilities for the world. They had a fresh sense of mystery, a strong sense of creativity, which brought more hope than they had ever had.

But they also saw the harsh truth of this new way of life. Simeon gave us the other side of the Christmas story before he departed. He wouldn't let us rest with the softness, the gentleness, the tenderness, and the peacefulness of the manger. Simeon told Mary about her son, "His life is going to cause much disruption in this world. He is going to bring a new way of being. He will challenge people's values. He will face opposition and upset people's lives. He is going to call them to live in ways that are not comfortable. And the suffering he will endure is going to pierce your heart like a sword." Stirring words for a new mother to hear, but these words cause us to ask, "Where is God in all of this?"

God is in the peacefulness and beauty of life to be sure, but he is also in the turmoil and ugliness of it. God is in the joys of our living but also in the sorrows. God is there when life is carefree and there when life is worrisome. God is there. This is what Simeon is saying to us about the good news coming to birth in the form of this tiny infant. Simeon and Anna see in that baby the power to make a difference in this world.

As we seek to have our faith deepened and our eyes sharpened, we can see through this lovely work of art hanging over the chancel, the intimacy that God wishes for us as depicted in that close connection between mother and child. We now have the possibility of seeing in this bread and this wine a new awareness of God's presence permeating our lives, as we are sent out from this church into the world around us. We now have eyes opened to see the face of Christ in the tear-stained and fear-ridden eyes of a child brought up in public housing. We are given new eyes with which to see because of the imaginative faith of Simeon and Anna. May their old eyes become our eyes this day, and may we be opened anew to see Christ's presence with us in every aspect of our lives. By God's grace, may we receive their example and be sent from this place to be Christ's people in this fear-ridden and hate-filled world. God is there.

A Person-to-Person Call

JOHN 1:43–51

The next day Jesus decided to go to Galilee. He found Philip and said to him, "Follow me." Now Philip was from Bethsaida, the city of Andrew and Peter. Philip found Nathanael and said to him, "We have found him about whom Moses in the law and also the prophets wrote, Jesus son of Joseph from Nazareth." Nathanael said to him, "Can anything good come out of Nazareth?" Philip said to him, "Come and see." When Jesus saw Nathanael coming toward him, he said of him, "Here is truly an Israelite in whom there is no deceit!" Nathanael asked him, "Where did you get to know me?" Jesus answered, "I saw you under the fig tree before Philip called you." Nathanael replied, "Rabbi, you are the Son of God! You are the King of Israel!" Jesus answered, "Do you believe because I told you that I saw you under the fig tree? You will see greater things than these." And he said to him, "Very truly, I tell you, you will see heaven opened and the angels of God ascending and descending upon the Son of Man."

*T*his season of Epiphany is a celebration of the joy of finding and being found. In this gospel we witness an odd encounter Jesus had with Philip and Nathanael. The New Testament mentions Philip and Nathanael only a few times, so they are relative strangers to us. Philip is from the hometown of Andrew and Peter in Bethsaida, a fishing village located at the mouth of the river Jordan on the edge of the Sea of Galilee. Bethsaida means "the city of the fishery," so Philip is probably a fisherman. Nathanael is from the small town of Cana, the same town of the wedding miracle. Philip and Nathanael were young men when they encountered Jesus, so they hadn't made much of an impact in their hometowns. But when they met Jesus, their lives were turned around. First of all, they were found. Philip and Nathanael had probably been followers of John the Baptizer, and their soul-searching had brought them together as friends. The Gospel tells us clearly that Jesus found Philip as he sensed in Philip a special quality which moved him to ask Philip to become his first disciple.

After Philip's experience with Jesus, he immediately went to find Nathanael sitting under a fig tree, where all devout Jewish people sat. Fig trees were massive trees in that time, so they provided heavily shaded and secluded solitary places for spiritual reflection. Nathanael was sitting under the tree, saying his prayers, reading his scriptures, and trying to discover what God wanted for his life. Philip draws Nathanael out of his solitude and tells him, "I found him; I found the one we have been looking for. He has found me and I am surprised that he found me and he is asking something of me. I want you to find him so he can find you too."

Nathanael doesn't believe the Messiah would come from the tiny obscure fishing village of Nazareth, so Philip tells him, "Come see for yourself. I think he can find you and I hope you can discover something about yourself as well." We can tell that Nathanael is a skeptical person, absolutely forthright in his questioning. More than a skeptic, however, Nathanael is a bigoted, prejudiced, biased cynic, unable to be found, unwilling to find out about himself. He reluctantly ventures out from under the shady fig tree to find Jesus, who makes his life anew.

As a result of their encounter with Jesus, Philip and Nathanael became two of the most powerful missionaries of the early church. They were ordinary people whom Jesus found, transformed by self-discovery brought about through their new relationship with the Lord Christ. Their lives bear testimony to the fact that they discovered possibilities they had never experienced before their encounter with Christ. These missionaries then spread the Gospel to the world.

How is the Gospel spread? It is spread strictly through people, those who find it and who are found by it. The Gospel dies if we don't share what we have found with those who are still looking. We are sometimes called into places we least expect, and we have our eyes and minds opened to opportunities we never envisioned.

This past week, District 7 school administrators and principals called one hundred and forty-five Spartanburg clergy to a meeting. Seven of us responded to the call and attended a meeting, where we were told that the schools need what church people have to give. And then began the long litany of cries by one principal after another, describing the needs in their schools. One principal stood and said, "We have no men in our entire school. We had one male teacher last year, but he was promoted to assistant principal. Our kitchen staff and maintenance personnel are all women. That's wonderful," she said, "but it is not enough. We have children in our school who know no men in their families and in their neighborhoods, and we need some men who are willing to give of themselves to let these children know that they matter enough to be given some time and attention. We are looking to you, we are calling on you, to help with children we cannot help enough by ourselves."

Another principal stood and told the story of a little boy who was sent to her office every day for the first couple of months of school. He was removed from class due to his disruptive behavior. With that little boy in the classroom, the teacher could not maintain the other children's attention and teach them. Day after day, the boy would disrupt class and be sent to the principal's office. She said, "After a while I began to discover what was going on. The child disrupted class so he could spend ninety minutes a day with me, where he received my undivided attention. That student put himself through the ridicule of his classmates so he could spend those precious ninety minutes per day in the security of my office. I asked a person to come and read to this child for an hour every day, and this student has not been sent to my office since that helpful volunteer has given the gift of time to that boy."

A cry has come to us, a cry as strong as that which came to us before we established St. Luke's Free Medical Clinic here in Spartanburg. This is not a cry for professionals; this is a cry to each one of us. Jesus went to ordinary people and called them into tasks they never thought they could fulfill. Nathanael was as scared as anyone who enters a classroom without teaching experience. Philip was probably scared as he set out on the first unknown steps of his missionary journeys. One of the truths in that encounter between Jesus, Philip, and Nathanael is this:

God does not call those who are fit; God makes fit those whom he calls. Every one of us in this church has something to offer these children who are deprived beyond our imagination, emotionally malnourished beyond our comprehension.

One of the greatest memories of my childhood is the gift of time my parents would spend reading to me. This is a gift that has never lost its value, even though I didn't know the meaning of the gift when it was given to me. There are hundreds of children at Mary H. Wright School who have never received that gift. On their behalf the challenge is laid before us. By God's grace, like Philip and Nathanael, may we take the risk of changing our minds beyond our prejudices, beyond our narrowness, to open our hearts and use them as conduits of Christ's love. In response to this call, may we have our wills forged like steel by the love of Christ, which has found us. Now we are called to find others who know it not. By God's grace, may we hear this call and be empowered to offer what is sorely needed. Amen.

The Growing Season

MATTHEW 4:12–23

Now when Jesus heard that John had been arrested, he withdrew to Galilee. He left Nazareth and made his home in Capernaum by the sea, in the territory of Zebulun and Naphtali, so that what had been spoken through the prophet Isaiah might be fulfilled: "Land of Zebulun, land of Naphtali, on the road by the sea, across the Jordan, Galilee of the Gentiles—the people who sat in darkness have seen a great light, and for those who sat in the region and shadow of death light has dawned." From that time Jesus began to proclaim, "Repent, for the kingdom of heaven has come near." As he walked by the Sea of Galilee, he saw two brothers, Simon, who is called Peter, and Andrew his brother, casting a net into the sea—for they were fishermen. And he said to them, "Follow me, and I will make you fish for people." Immediately they left their nets and followed him. As he went from there, he saw two other brothers, James son of Zebedee and his brother John, in the boat with their father Zebedee, mending their nets, and he called them. Immediately they left the boat and their father, and followed him. Jesus went throughout Galilee, teaching in their synagogues and proclaiming the good news of the kingdom and curing every disease and every sickness among the people.

Well, here we are again, right in the middle of Epiphany, that six-week segment of the Christian year which might get lost in the shuffle because it is sandwiched in between the great celebration of Christmas and the very emotional and demanding season of Lent and the glorious joyful season of Easter. So we almost forget about Epiphany. It is a short season, but to me it is the pivotal season in the Christian year because of the fact that it brings us face to face with the question of what our mission in life is to be. Epiphany season is the missionary season of the church. It is the growing season and that is why our liturgical color has changed to green. This is a wonderful time of the year, because to me it means more than growth and greenness. It is a season of searching.

It is a season of new revelations and fresh insights and deepened understanding. It is a time for new ways of perceiving life, ourselves, and our ministry in life. And of course the main story of the Epiphany is the story of the three magi—wise men or kings—who were on a journey.

They had left everything familiar behind, everything comfortable, just like the fishermen in today's Gospel were called to do. They dared to trust God's guidance and travel out into the unknown, led by the wondrous star as they wandered through the darkness in a strange land. In this process they experienced some revelations which were startling to them, totally life-changing. This is a season of pilgrimage, a season of searching. A time for asking new questions and being given new answers, and having our minds and our hearts opened with fresh revelations which God has in store for each one of us.

Epiphany is a wonderful time in the Church of the Advent to launch a new venture. Today we begin Project Epiphany. You will be hearing much about this new project in the months ahead, because we are not going to spend simply six weeks in Epiphany. We are going to spend the first six months of this year (1999) in our Epiphany journey. We are going to be opening ourselves to new revelations from God in terms of what God is calling us to be as his people in this time and in this place. What does the future hold for us in terms of what God is going to show us and expect of us? Project Epiphany begins this morning, but this venture does not simply spring up out of nowhere. Three years of hard work have gone into preparation for this effort. Three years ago I called together all of the former senior wardens of this congregation and asked them to pool their wisdom, their commitment, and their resources to launch us into the future. Out of that meeting came a strategic planning committee. Many more people became involved and from this small gathering we are brought today to Project Epiphany.

We have hired a consultant to guide us like that bright star led those original wise men. We brought in someone from afar who knows very little about us but will help us ask the right questions about ourselves. He will be God's gift to us at this critical moment in our life.

So as we begin this Epiphany pilgrimage together, opening ourselves to new revelations, we begin our discernment on the basis of some learnings which come directly from the life and ministry of our Lord himself. As we seek to be the body of Christ in this place, we are not simply going to be at the mercy of our own biases, whims, and wishes. We are going to be reflecting on our life against the backdrop of at least four areas of understanding which Jesus brought to us.

First, we will concentrate on Jesus as High Priest and Celebrant, and assess the importance of worship in our congregation. How clearly do we proclaim the Gospel in this place? How effectively do we share this Gospel with people who have not yet heard it? Next, we are going to focus on Jesus as Pastor and Comforter. In light of this attribute of our Lord's life, we will ask ourselves how well we care for one another. How intent are we on healing one another from the hurts which life brings to us all? Then we will reflect on Jesus as Prophet and Servant, as he calls us out of those familiar, comfortable places in our lives to enter into the darkness and the pain of the world beyond the walls of this parish. What will we be challenged to become as we follow our Lord as prophet and servant? And finally, we will turn our attention to Jesus as Teacher and Guide. Here we will ask ourselves how effective we are in educating one another in the faith, nurturing one another in our spiritual growth, and equipping one another for ministry in the world.

So you can see that we are going to look at the total life of our parish against the backdrop of these aspects of our Lord's life which have been revealed to us. The questions are going to call from us ministry opportunities which we cannot even begin to envision right now. Above all, we are going to shape our ecclesiology according to our Christology. So we have a mighty challenge before us in these next six months.

Your clergy, your vestry, the leaders of the project have committed themselves to this effort, and my fervent hope is to have everyone in this congregation assume a vital role in this effort as it unfolds. We need all of our insights; we need all of our expectations; we need all of our questions, so that God may speak through all of us to each of us. To that end, each of you received a piece of paper when you came in to church today. On it are listed five aspects of our life together. I want you to check one of these areas in which you have vital concern, interest, questions, experience, or giftedness. Once you indicate your choice, you will receive a call from one of your vestry about forming reflection groups, which will then meet throughout the parish for the next several months. Our consultant will have a series of questions for each of us to answer, so there will be a common focus resulting from these gatherings. But we need to have your response, so that we may create a common vision to guide us into our future.

I have prepared scriptural reflections for each of our gatherings so that all of our discussions will begin with a clear understanding of what the Bible tells us about these special attributes of our Lord's life. We will spend much time thinking, studying, reflecting, searching, journeying, and opening ourselves to new revelations and new insights. We will challenge one another. We will uphold one another. We will appreciate each other. We will call each other to venture beyond the place we are now. As we examine the mission imperatives which grow from our Lord's example, we will become a parish of miraculous expectations.We will then proceed into the last half of this year with a clear vision and full knowledge of the life God is calling this congregation to live in this time.

We stand on the cusp of a new century, a new millennium. Only God knows at this point the shape of this vision. But during Project Epiphany we will be called together to dream big dreams and see expansive visions. We will be committing ourselves to following the wondrous star which may lead us into the unfamiliar, but will eventually lead us to new and fresh understanding of what it means to be willing to follow Christ in this time and place.

Therefore, I ask you to make your Epiphany commitment today by choosing one of these areas of our parish life to evaluate and dream about: worship, pastoral care, servanthood in the world, Christian nurture, and stewardship. In so doing, you will become a fellow pilgrim, and you will share in the joy of all the revelations God will give to all of us. Above all, I want this effort to be undergirded by prayer, so that even the people in our parish who are homebound and cannot participate in these gatherings can be praying for the rest of us who still have the blessing of our health and mobility. In this way, no one will be left out of this venture. The prayer I want to use in each gathering is found in the Book of Common Prayer. It is taken from the Solemn Collects of Good Friday. It is also the prayer used at the ordination of clergy. Each one of us has been ordained to ministry. This is what our baptism does for us. So this is the prayer which will be prayed over every meeting of our folks during the next six months.

O God of unchangeable power and eternal light: Look favorably on your whole Church, that wonderful and sacred mystery; by the effectual working of your providence, carry out in tranquility the plan of salvation; let the whole world see and know that things which were cast down are being raised up, and things which had grown old are being made new, and that all things are being brought to their perfection by him through whom all things were made, your Son Jesus Christ our Lord; who lives and reigns with you, in the unity of the Holy Spirit, one God, for ever and ever. Amen.

*P*ieces of Clay

Jesus proclaimed the radical inclusiveness of God's grace. That idea enraged people then, and if we take it seriously, it is liable to enrage us today. The anger being generated by the conflict we in the church are living through in 2004 is based on whether or not we believe that God's grace is radically inclusive. This is the bottom line. What matters is not who the people are, what they do, or how they live. What matters is whether or not we believe in the fact that God's grace is given to all of us freely. We do not earn it. Jesus said to those people in his own hometown, "God's grace is reserved for those folks beyond you and not just for you." Jesus was indicating that your God is too small if you only see God's grace reserved for yourself.

—

From our Native American culture comes a wonderful story. One day an old man and his grandson are floating the great river. During a quiet and peaceful part of the journey, the grandfather starts to tell the grandson about the most agonizing moment in his life when his wife suddenly died of a strange disease. He told of how painful his life had been since that time. He said to his grandson that from the moment of his wife's death there had been a war in his heart between two wolves. One wolf was mean, vengeful, angry, and hopeless. The other wolf was loving, tender, compassionate, peaceful, and hopeful. They paddled on a little more and finally the grandson asked, "Grandfather, which of the wolves is going to win that war?" And the grandfather quietly said, "The one I feed."

We have a choice, my friends. Which wolf do we feed? Do

we live in the aftermath of September 11 as vengeful, angry, hopeless, insecure, and in despair? Or do we live as tender, compassionate, loving, redemptive people who are beacons of hope to a dark world?

———

I believe the spiritual vitality of the church is not to be measured by the size of its budget, its buildings, its membership, or its staff. Spiritual vitality of any congregation is to be measured by our response to this question: How many have you healed? By God's grace may we have the wisdom, compassion, and endurance to hold up before ourselves this question which is our main challenge as we enter into our future. How many have you healed?

———

As we celebrate our 150-year anniversary as a congregation, we are being pulled beyond where we are into something new. This shouldn't really distress us too much, because we are the people of The Advent. We are people who are called together and named to be those who should expect the new; people who wait for God's truth to open up to us in ways we have not yet perceived; to be certainly willing to share what we have been given out of our history. But we are creating history ourselves at this moment, and the people who will celebrate the liturgy here 150 years from now, will look back upon us as people of The Advent who accepted our challenge to be Christ's people in this time. We will be remembered as instruments of Christ's love, healing, and peace; as people who were willing to take risks, to go beyond the familiar, beyond what we can control, and place ourselves in the hands of God, opening our ears, our minds, and our hearts to a new voice of Christ which will lead us to be his people in a brand new way.

Lent

Lent is a time of purification of our spirits, similar to the bisque firing of the pot in the heat of the kiln, which rids the pot of excess moisture and impurities.

PRAYER FOR LENT: Holy God, when we wander from the way, call us back. When we stray from the truth, redirect us. When we do not live life to the full, inspire and refresh us. Help us to follow more closely the one who is the way, the truth, and the life, your son Jesus Christ, our Lord. AMEN

A Pruning and Thinning Time

MATTHEW 6:5–6, 16–21

"And whenever you pray, do not be like the hypocrites; for they love to stand and pray in the synagogues and at the street corners, so that they may be seen by others. Truly I tell you, they have received their reward. But whenever you pray, go into your room and shut the door and pray to your Father who is in secret; and your Father who sees in secret will reward you. And whenever you fast, do not look dismal, like the hypocrites, for they disfigure their faces so as to show others that they are fasting. Truly I tell you, they have received their reward. But when you fast put oil on your head and wash your face, so that your fasting may be seen not by others but by your Father who is in secret; and your Father who sees in secret will reward you. Do not store up for yourselves treasures on earth, where moth and rust consume and where thieves break in and steal; but store up for yourselves treasures in heaven, where neither moth nor rust consumes and where thieves do not break in and steal. For where your treasure is, there your heart will be also."

It seems mighty strange to other denominations, these customs we follow in liturgical churches. In fact, it took the church itself about six hundred years to figure it all out. Easter, as we know, always has been the principal day of worship, and every Sunday takes its pattern from the day of the Resurrection. But eventually people started to see that it was necessary to establish a period of preparation for this high feast day. Our Jewish forebears always gave great importance to preparation for a major religious event, so the early Christian leaders decided that probably it would be spiritually beneficial to designate forty hours before Easter to prepare for this great celebration, too.

As time passed people added certain days and the season of preparation increased to seven days. Then it became thirty days, then thirty-five days. Finally somebody suggested that since Jesus was in the wilderness for forty days, it would be appropriate to set aside forty days to prepare for Easter, and those forty days began to be called Lent.

It took nearly three hundred years to develop this under-standing. Then the forty days became a source of debate. People wondered about Easter. Since Easter is not a day of fasting, and Sunday is not a day of fasting, they began to subtract all the Sundays. Finally Pope Gregory the Great decided to put an end to the endless debate. "There will be forty days of preparation which we will call Lent, and we will begin it on a Wednesday, not a Sunday," he declared. So in the latter part of the sixth century, this period of time was prescribed and this day was set aside. It took another several hundred years for liturgies to be formed around this day.

So it is no wonder people outside our denomination are confused. It has taken a long time to get any sense of understanding about the celebration we call Ash Wednesday. There are many layers of meaning packed into this special day. In times past, people saw Ash Wednesday as a day to mourn their sinfulness. When Puritanism dominated theology, the focus was on the total depravity of human beings—our absolute worthlessness—on Ash Wednesday. Thank goodness that focus has changed. But throughout all of these fourteen hundred years of development, one theme has run throughout, the theme of fasting.

In this Gospel account for today we hear Jesus talking about the three pillars of Judaism: *alms giving*, which has to do with generosity of self; *prayer*, which has to do with acknowledging our dependence upon God; and *fasting,* which has to do with a spiritual house-cleaning we are called to do regularly.

Fasting has been vastly misunderstood across Christendom. Many denominations still focus on this part of Christian discipline as necessary to our soul's health. But on this day fasting is held up before us as the spiritual ideal. When we consider fasting though, I hope we will look at it in a way other than simply depriving ourselves of something external. This time we are entering into is also a time of growth, a time of renewal, a time of refreshment, a time of possibilities being developed in our own spiritual lives. Fasting, to me, has an important part to play in our own spiritual growth.

This year the whole aspect of fasting means more to me because of a series of new personal discoveries. I have been privileged to become a part of a master gardening program here in Spartanburg. I have always loved to dig in the dirt, but I never knew what made soil soil and what made it grow things sometimes and what made it kill things sometimes. Now I know. Several important elements of effective gardening are analyzing and amending the soil and pruning and thinning plants.

For me this year, Ash Wednesday is the day of taking a soil test of my soul. Have you ever taken a soil test? If you haven't, you have probably wasted a lot of plants like I have. Maybe you thought that dirt could naturally grow plants, but it won't. All soil needs regular analysis and amending. Dirt is not just dirt. Likewise, our lives need evaluation and nutrients added to them all the time, but I'm afraid that we live in a time in our society which encourages us to add only clutter to our lives.

Today as we take a soil test of our soul, it is also important for us to learn about the essential practice of pruning and thinning which enables plants to thrive. What in our lives needs pruning this day? What needs thinning? The purpose of pruning and thinning is not just to shape a lovely bush. Thinning and pruning allow air to flow through a plant so that water dries quickly enough to prevent insects and diseases from damaging the plant. Thinning and pruning allow sun to touch the base of the plant so that it can receive the proper nutrients that it needs to flourish. I hope this Lent will be a time of thinning and pruning as you decide what in your life is a sucker. Do you know anything about suckers? Suckers are sprouts that grow out of branches or roots. They look lovely, but they produce nothing. They only take precious energy from the plant and reduce its ability to produce beautiful flowers and delicious fruit. Our lives have too many suckers attached to them, which can sap our energy and resources without producing fruitful living.

What is it today that needs pruning and thinning from our life? That's a very serious question to think about in terms of fasting. I know we have already probably begun to think about all those things we are going to give up for Lent—like chocolate, chewing gum, watermelon, alcohol, and all those things that have nothing to do with our soul's nourishment. But what do we need to stop doing that prohibits the *Christ-likeness* in all of us from being expressed?

I have studied behavior change most of my life, and I have learned much from experts who devote their entire careers to this topic. Studies indicate clearly that if we are serious about making changes in behavior we need to be as specific as we can be. It is not going to be enough for us to go out of here full of inspiration, saying, "I'm going to be a brand new person, and I'm going to do *everything* differently." We would be demoralized before we got our car out of the parking lot. We need to be specific about changes, which must happen to improve our soul's health.

The fasting, then, is the thinning and the pruning. The feasting is adding nutrients to our soul's life so that we may grow into the people God created us to become. Lent is not a time to wallow in our imperfection, our sinfulness, our inadequacy, and our worthlessness. This is a time for us to examine the potential that has been thwarted in our lives. Lent can be an uncomfortable time; self-examination is never easy for any of us. We learned long ago from Socrates that the unexamined life is not worth living, and Jesus kept talking over and over about repentance, which has to do with self-examination, too.

I have learned from my alcoholic friends about the absolute necessity of a fearless moral inventory. No one of us can do a fearless moral inventory with comfort and ease. Yet taking an honest inward look, uncomfortable as it may be, is a prerequisite to positive behavior change and growth. Thinning and pruning hurts. But it takes the honest recognition of what is wrong about our life before we can make it right.

So, my friends, I pray that this will be forty days of examination in terms of where your suckers are, in terms of what needs thinning and pruning out of your life, and what needs to be added to your life so that the soil of your soul will be rich and fertile, enabling you to grow into the lovely creature God has created you to be.

By God's grace, may we all be willing to be discomforted, to take a close look, to make some sharp cuts, and add some necessary nutrients to the soil of our soul.

Because Jesus Wept

JOHN 11:17–44

When Jesus arrived, he found that Lazarus had already been in the tomb four days. Now Bethany was near Jerusalem, some two miles away, and many of the Jews had come to Martha and Mary to console them about their brother. When Martha heard that Jesus was coming, she went and met him, while Mary stayed at home. Martha said to Jesus, "Lord, if you had been here, my brother would not have died. But even now I know that God will give you whatever you ask of him." Jesus said to her, "Your brother will rise again." Martha said to him, "I know that he will rise again in the resurrection on the last day." Jesus said to her, "I am the resurrection and the life. Those who believe in me, even though they die, will live, and everyone who lives and believes in me will never die. Do you believe this?" She said to him, "Yes, Lord, I believe that you are the Messiah, the Son of God, the one coming into the world." When she had said this, she went back and called her sister Mary, and told her privately, "The Teacher is here and is calling for you." And when she heard it, she got up quickly and went to him. Now Jesus had not yet come to the village but was still at the place where Martha had met him. The Jews who were with her in the house, consoling her, saw Mary get up quickly and go out. They followed her because they thought that she was going to the tomb to weep there. When Mary came where Jesus was and saw him, she knelt at his feet and said to him, "Lord, if you had been here, my brother would not have died." When Jesus saw her weeping, and the Jews that came with her also weeping, he was greatly disturbed in spirit and deeply moved. He said, "Where have you laid him?" They said to him, "Lord, come and see." Jesus began to weep. So the Jews said, "See how he loved him!" But some of them said, "Could not he who opened the eyes of the blind man have kept this man from dying?" Then Jesus, again greatly disturbed, came to the tomb. It was a cave, and a stone was lying against it. Jesus said, "Take away the stone." Martha, the sister of the dead man, said to him, "Lord, already there is a stench because he has been dead four days." Jesus said to her, "Did I not tell you that if you believed, you would see the glory of God?" So they took away the stone. And Jesus looked upward and said, "Father, I thank you for having heard me. I knew that you always hear me, but I have said this for the sake of the crowd standing here, so that they may believe that you have sent me." When he had said this, he cried with a loud voice, "Lazarus, come out!" The dead man came out, his hands and feet bound with strips of cloth, and his face wrapped in a cloth. Jesus said to them, "Unbind him, and let him go."

Only John records the story of the raising of Lazarus from the dead. That the three Synoptic Gospels paid no attention to it has troubled scholars over the centuries. How could an event this dramatic have escaped the memories of the first three Gospel writers?

But for John, this was a pivotal experience in Jesus' life, and it should be a pivotal event in our own spiritual journey too.

John began his marvelous way of recounting Jesus' ministry with his first miracle, which took place at a wedding in Cana of Galilee. There as the great celebrant, he was in a house filled with joy and with a group of people whose hearts were filled with joy. Jesus even added to the joy by creating more wine out of the water jugs that were left behind in the kitchen.

Yes, his first miracle took place in a heart full of joy and a house full of gladness. But his last miracle took place in an empty house. The man of the house had died and had been taken away, leaving behind the empty hearts of his sisters.

What do these two miracles say to us? First of all, we are told that Jesus is a celebrant in our lives, but he is also a suffering servant with us as we face death in all its forms.

This congregation has been swamped by death lately. Fourteen people have died in the last three months. We have an unprecedented number of men out of work for the first time in their lives, helplessly trying to find their way back into a very unresponsive job market. We have many people in our congregation who have lost everything that has given their lives a sense of security. They have lost their marriages; they have lost their homes; they have lost their own sense of who they are. With their vocations now in jeopardy, they have lost all of the things which used to give life meaning. Many of us in this congregation wonder if there will ever be any joy in our lives again.

I have in my office two artistic creations. One of them is very simple; it's a pencil drawing of the laughing Christ. Most of the Gospel writers don't even tell us that Jesus ever smiled, much less laughed. But I can imagine Jesus laughing with the family at that wedding in Cana, and I can imagine how he laughed when he brought out the best wine at the last. In the laughing Christ, Jesus has his head back, mouth open, in a roaring belly laugh—a wonderful expression of the Jesus who celebrates with us in the joys of our living!

But hanging opposite that drawing on my wall is a wood carving, a wood carving of a head-down, eyes-closed, crown-of-thorns-covered, man-of-sorrows suffering servant. This Jesus not only celebrates our joys, but shares our deepest sorrows. This is where we find our Lord in this Gospel, sharing our deepest sorrow. The situation is a poignant one. Lazarus was a close friend of Jesus; some scholars even say that Lazarus was the beloved disciple, not St. John. Some think that Jesus grew up with Lazarus, and that they played together as boys. One thing we do know is that Jesus always used the home of Mary and Martha and Lazarus as his retreat. It was in the suburbs, just a short walk outside the walls of the big city of Jerusalem, and Jesus often went there for quiet times so he could let his hair down literally and figuratively…a place where he could take off his sandals and put his feet on the table…where he didn't have to be on guard and worry about how people were going to respond to what he said and what he did. He could go there and simply relax with Mary and Martha and Lazarus.

And now, as he came to this place for a retreat once again, he found that his closest friend, Lazarus, had died and had been in a tomb four days—a concrete expression that Jesus was confronting death. The Jewish theology of life after death was that the person's spirit hovered over the body for three days;

then on the fourth day it departed, leaving the body in total isolation. Lazarus had been there four days.

There are many perplexities about what happened at that moment in that empty house with that empty chair and those empty hearts. I don't begin to pretend to explain all the mysteries of the raising of Lazarus. But a couple of things jump out at me and give my life some mooring, give my life some base, provide some sense of an anchor to hold onto when life is shifting and changing all around me.

The first thing is this: the shortest verse in scripture is contained in this Gospel. Four words find their way into this translation; King James has only two: "Jesus wept." "Jesus began to weep," says our translation today. I remember when I was a boy in Sunday school; the teacher would always make us recite a verse of scripture when she would take roll. Being a smart aleck, I would always quote the shortest verse in the Bible. Sunday after Sunday I would say, "Jesus wept." That verse of scripture got me by for a long time. Little did I know that I was imprinting on my heart and soul a truth which would sustain me in my days of sharing all kinds of sorrow and heartbreak with others.

The fact that Jesus wept was preposterous to a Greek, and John was writing this Gospel primarily to Greek people. Greeks believed that God was passionless, compassionless, and emotionless. They believed that God could not *feel* in response to whatever happened in human life. Feeling emotion would mean that human beings could affect God and, therefore, have some control over him and his emotional swings. It really was heresy that Jesus wept, heresy for two reasons. If the Greeks did believe that Jesus was God incarnate, the fact that he cried was a theological heresy because God did not get moved by human events. Secondly, to say that a man could cry was probably even more a psychological heresy than a theological one, because in our society today men just don't cry. Crying is a sign that we are weak, that something is wrong; we ought to be able to stand up and face our problems and not let anybody see where we hurt.

We have our Lord's model as the way to be a man. Jesus modeled the fact that we are to be moved deeply by life and respond to it with our tears. The Greek word used in this Gospel—that Jesus was deeply moved in his spirit—is hard to translate because the original Greek meaning was used for a grunt that a horse made when it was mortally wounded. Jesus groaned that deeply; he felt pain so strongly that he could find no words to express it. Tears were the best expression of his sadness, and his tears flowed freely, thank God.

Jesus joins us in our sorrow, and he hurts with us; that's good news to me. It gives some sense of meaning to know that we don't suffer alone, no matter what we have lost. The One whom we follow, obey, and worship is the One who joins us in the midst of our pain and embraces that pain with us.

Two other things stand out in this Gospel as good news to me. Remember what Jesus did when he approached the tomb? Through his tears and with his voice cracking in his own grief, he said to the community of people standing outside that tomb, "Would someone please roll away that stone from the door of the tomb for me?" It was a custom in those days to bury people in caves, either caves dug by human beings or natural caves. Shelves were put inside these caves, and when bodies were stacked four or five high, a stone was pushed up to the door to keep wild creatures and predators from coming in and defacing the bodies. So Jesus asked someone in the crowd to roll away the stone. We are called to be participants in miracles; we are called to be stone rollers.

Jesus certainly could have pushed that stone away. He had plenty of power to do that. If he could raise a person from the dead, he could remove a stone. But he invited the community to be part of the miracle of new life, thereby calling each one of us to be a stone roller in other people's lives, too.

We are called to push away whatever it is that stands in the way of life for people. We are called to push that stone away to give people a chance to breathe some fresh air and see some light and some hope and some joy, and feel some warmth. We need to push the stone away so that people don't feel isolated anymore.

Can you imagine the gasp of the crowd as Jesus called Lazarus to come out, and they saw a dead man emerge from the mouth of that cave? "Some of you go over there and take off those grave bindings," he instructed. It was a Jewish custom to bind the body as tightly as it could be bound with linen wrappings. The body was bound; the feet were bound; the head was bound separately. Imagine the astonishment of the crowd when Lazarus was standing raggedly at the mouth of that cave, still constrained by the grave bindings! "Go and unwrap him," Jesus said.

We are not only called to be stone rollers, but we are also called to be unravelers of whatever it is that binds people up. If it's fear, if it's anxiety, if it's hopelessness, if it's grief, if it's despair, if it's rage—no matter what it is that cuts us off from life—we are called as Christ's followers to unbind people and to let them go to live the life, the resurrected life, that Jesus came to bring…a resurrected life here and now, not just in the hereafter.

This is Jesus' great proclamation to Mary and Martha. The Resurrection is here and now, and God wills new and abundant life for each of us at this moment.

No matter what kinds of stones we have rolled up against the face of our life, no matter what kind of bondage we may find ourselves in, we share the good news in the face of the deaths we experience that there is hope for us regardless of the death. The loss we may experience at this moment comes with God's promise of new life, not just out there in the hereafter, but right here and right now.

Thanks be to God for the gift of this promise. Amen.

All You (N)ever Needed

LUKE 4:1–13

After his baptism, Jesus, full of the Holy Spirit, returned from the Jordan and was led by the Spirit in the wilderness, where for forty days he was tempted by the devil. He ate nothing at all during those days, and when they were over, he was famished. The devil said to him, "If you are the Son of God, command this stone to become a loaf of bread." Jesus answered him, "It is written, 'One does not live by bread alone.'" Then the devil led him up and showed him in an instant all the kingdoms of the world. And the devil said to him, "To you I will give their glory and all this authority; for it has been given over to me, and I give it to anyone I please. If you, then, will worship me, it will all be yours." Jesus answered him, "It is written, 'Worship the Lord your God, and serve only him.'" Then the devil took him to Jerusalem, and placed him on the pinnacle of the temple, saying to him, "If you are the Son of God, throw yourself down from here, for it is written, 'He will command his angels concerning you to protect you, and on their hands they will bear you up, so that you will not dash foot against a stone.'" Jesus answered him, "It is said, 'Do not put the Lord your God to the test.'" When the devil had finished every test, he departed from him until an opportune time.

*T*oday we take more steps in this journey called life. This whole season of Lent is about a journey or a hike or a pilgrimage of moving from one place to another. The destination of this season is renewal and revival and transformation; it is a new sense of who we are and what we are called to be in this life. This is the process of Lent, but it is really the process of life for us, isn't it, that we are always moving on.

It's not a comfortable place to be, as we see in the life of our Lord in this gospel reading. Jesus was not in a place he wanted to go. He was led there. One of the Gospel writers said he was pushed there, driven there, as though he somewhat resisted being in Ishaman. After all, Ishaman was the place called the devastation, the desert, the wilderness, the most barren place in the world between the Dead Sea and the central plateau of Palestine—a forbidding, dangerous, barren place.

This story has to be one that Jesus told from his own experience. Since no one was with him, nobody could give an eyewitness account or be scribbling down notes about what he was saying or what he was doing. He was all by himself in this deserted place, this abandoned place.

I can imagine Jesus sitting around the campfire one night with his friends, telling them about his own struggle of soul. He wanted them to know what he went through in the wilderness so they could understand him better and gain some insight into themselves as well. Jesus was talking about real life temptations here. This was no shadowboxing. This was no sham battle. He was not pretending to struggle. He was struggling mightily with some things that were tearing at his heart, his mind, and his soul. These temptations were real. They were tests more than they were temptations, but the struggle was real.

There is an amazing contrast between that lush, cool, moist

Jordan River valley, and a few steps away that barren, parched, fire furnace of a desert. Jesus was still dripping wet from his baptism when he came out of the water and entered that forbidden environment all by himself. It was not self-evident to Jesus who he was to be when he came out of the water. It's obvious from this story that he had to go and struggle to find out who it was he was called to be, who it was to be the Son of God, who it was to be Messiah.

He had to go and face some choices, some tough choices. Because of the power he had, the danger he brought to life was great, and he knew that. So he had to go and struggle for a while with the question of how he was to use his power.

Here he was, a long time with nothing to eat. The Gospel account says he was famished, beginning to wonder whether he could stand up to this ordeal or not. He was beginning to wonder about himself. Do you notice in there the word "if" recurring? Jesus was beginning to wonder if he was the Son of God. What did that call forth from him? What did that demand of him? Am I capable of handling whatever will be asked of me? he wondered.

We, too, have self-doubts when we come to these defining moments, don't we? We wonder who we are. We wonder if we can stand it. We wonder if we can endure. We have all kinds of questions about ourselves every day if we are honest about taking life seriously. And here was Jesus, famished and fatigued, struggling within himself with a powerful test. The tester said to him, "Look around you. See all of those neat little limestones there? They look like little loaves of bread, don't they? Well, pick one up. You've got the power to turn this stone into something to eat and ease the gnawing in your own stomach." Jesus was mightily tempted to use his power in that way, but he didn't. He didn't because he knew something about himself, and he knows something about us as well—that nothing material in this life can satisfy our soul's desire.

Jesus almost succumbed to this temptation when he took the piece of rock and almost turned it into a delicious biscuit. He knew that if he yielded at that moment, the rest of his life would be spent seeking ultimate value in things, material and physical things, and he knew that would not satisfy his deepest hunger.

If you want to read a Jewish account of this kind of struggle in all of us, Rabbi Harold Kushner has written a wonderful book entitled *When All You Ever Needed Isn't Enough*. He says we struggle all the time with the obsession with things, thinking that if we can just acquire enough, accumulate enough, then certainly the restlessness in our souls will be put to rest. We know the futility of this frantic search. The insatiability in all of us wants more, yet we still feel the same kind of gnawing restlessness in the depth of our soul.

Jesus was able to check himself at this point and say to himself that only God can supply what our souls need, no matter how strongly our stomachs may gnaw at us. As soon as he put that test to rest he momentarily faced another one. This temptation is a little more seductive than the first one, a little more complicated. "What you need to do is make sure that you protect yourself from all harm," the tempter said. "Make sure your life is absolutely secure. Make sure you have control of everything, that you know the outcome of every action you are going to perform. Make sure you protect yourself; worship security."

This one really beguiles us. We all have so much anxiety over things we cannot control. We somehow think that if we are good enough and faithful, then certainly we are going to be immune to all those "slings and arrows of outrageous fortune." Certainly we will have good health; certainly we will have good wealth; certainly we will have good relationships; certainly everything will turn out all right. If we are just good enough, God will bless us with the assurance. Not so. Jesus knew that. We are spiritual animals, subject to all of the diseases and the accidents and the tragedies life has to offer. No one of us will ever be immune to this reality. If we worship security—keeping everything peaceful and protected—we are going to be continually living in fear because there is no way we can accomplish that. We are also going to rob ourselves of another thing Jesus knew about in this test. We will never find meaning in suffering if we see it as outside God's presence with us.

Jesus chose the way of suffering, not the way of protection. He chose to be a vulnerable human being. He chose to give up trying to protect himself against every harm.

The third test is the toughest of all. It's the temptation of power, authority, prestige, success, and control over other people. "I will give you control over the whole world and everybody in it. You've got the power to manage all that," the tempter promised. Jesus began to be very uneasy with the tension in himself. He realized that once he began to have power over other people, he would turn people into things, not creatures of God. At that moment in his life, he decided to move away from the love of power to the power of love. Living out of the power of love rather than the love of power. It's as different as that lush Jordan River valley and that dry, parched, deserted place.

Every one of us has a unique struggle in this life. We all have our own temptations and our own tests. We are all going to make the Lenten journey differently. But I would bet that we could find ourselves somewhere within the framework of these three tests which our Lord faced. As I face those tests in my own life, it is comforting to know that God was present and just as real in that deserted place as he was in that lush valley, and that God will not abandon us to wilderness so that we are left there to struggle on our own.

This is what the Lenten journey is all about. As we come face to face with ourselves and boldly face our ever-present temptations, we know that somehow Jesus joins us in our journey because he has made the same journey before us. He knows what it is to struggle and to suffer and to be in doubt and to wonder, and to feel the tension of so many things pulling at him at the same time.

As you make your journey this year, I hope you will be aware of Christ's example *before* you, and I hope you will be comforted by God's presence *with* you. I invite you to join the struggle…to be a part of the journey…to move from this place to someplace else so that Easter morn may be a true day of revival and renewal and new life for you all.

For Her, I Will Do Anything

MARK 8:31–38

Jesus began to teach his disciples that the Son of Man must undergo great suffering, and be rejected by the elders, the chief priests, and the scribes, and be killed, and after three days rise again. He said all this quite openly. And Peter took him aside and began to rebuke him. But turning and looking at his disciples, he rebuked Peter and said, "Get behind me, Satan! For you are setting your mind not on divine things but on human things." He called the crowd with his disciples, and said to them, "If any want to become my followers, let them deny themselves and take up their cross and follow me. For those who want to save their life will lose it, and those who lose their life for my sake, and for the sake of the Gospel, will save it. For what will it profit them to gain the whole world and forfeit their life? Indeed, what can they give in return for their life? Those who are ashamed of me and of my words in this adulterous and sinful generation, of them the Son of Man will also be ashamed when he comes in the glory of his Father with the holy angels."

*T*oday we get to the heart of the matter. We find the central core of meaning, the central core of Christian truth about what it means to be a follower of our Lord Jesus Christ.

Mark's words are hard words; they were hard words to hear then, and they are hard words for us to hear today. They are hard words because they are words of suffering, words of sacrifice, words of self-denial, words of taking up a cross. Those are the kinds of words which make us cringe when we wonder, Is that being asked of me?

Yes, it is. It was asked of our Lord's followers back in the days when he walked the earth. It is true for us who walk the earth in his stead now. We are those who are called to suffer, to sacrifice, to deny, and to take up a cross.

Peter couldn't bear to hear those words. He couldn't bear it for a couple of reasons. First of all, he didn't want to think that his beloved friend and Lord was about to undergo such agony, and he wanted to do everything he could to protect Jesus from what he was predicting for himself. But more importantly, Peter really didn't want to face up to this truth for himself. It bothered him about Jesus, but it bothered him even more about himself…this idea of suffering and sacrifice.

Jesus had been with his disciples almost three years—every day, day in and day out. They had watched him do his marvelous works; they had heard him preach; they had sat at his feet as their teacher and rabbi. But Mark tells us that at the end of all their experiences together, Jesus had to say those words over and over again. Mark's wording is subtle; the real translation should be "Jesus kept on saying it to them as plain as he could…over and over…because every time, they resisted hearing." When he would try to say it another way in order to get the truth home, Jesus would encounter the same kind of resistance, the same glazed eyes, the same furrowed brow, the same shaking of the head.

Peter was always the outspoken one. He probably spoke for

the group when he said, "Lord, this just cannot happen to *you*, and I don't want it to happen to *me* either." Jesus had an almost violent response to his closest friend, Peter. It's almost as though he pushed him aside, bored a hole in him with his eyes and told him that his thinking was not right, that he needed to get out of the way because he was an impediment to the truth. When Jesus saw that he wasn't getting through to his closest twelve friends, Mark tells us that Jesus called the whole crowd in and then began to tighten down even more. Jesus told all of the people there what it was going to be like to be his follower. The words our Lord speaks to us today are not just for the ordained. They are not just for those who have been appointed for a special task or ministry in life. Jesus looked beyond the first twelve whom he anointed and appointed for a special ministry, and drew the whole crowd in. He drew you in; he drew me in. "Now, here is how it is," he said. "If you are going to be serious about being a follower of mine, you are going to be called to suffer, to sacrifice, to deny, and to take up a cross."

Peter probably speaks for all of us. "God forbid, Lord. This cannot be true for you or for me." But it is. Now we come to the heart of the matter. The words "deny" and "cross" are words that are very easily misunderstood. When Jesus said, "Deny yourself," he didn't mean that you are to put yourself down, to hate yourself, to think poorly of yourself, or to neglect yourself. The real translation of the word to "deny" is to "let him make himself a stranger to himself." Or to put it another way, "let him be able to say no to his own needs." Now that's a pretty clear translation, isn't it? Deny yourself; make yourself a stranger to yourself. Be able to say no to your own needs enough to take on the needs of others. That's what the word "cross" means. It's a voluntary taking on of the burdens of other people.

Many of us misunderstand the word "cross." We think about a calamity as a cross we are given to bear. This isn't accurate. We think about grief from a terrible loss that we are feeling as a cross we have to bear. That isn't what it means. We sometimes think in terms of our own imperfections, our anger, or our impatience as crosses we have to bear. This isn't correct, because we don't have any choice in those things.

A *cross* is something that we make a choice for—to take upon ourselves the burden of other people. When Jesus was talking to those people then and talking to us today, he was not asking that we would do one thing that he was not willing to do himself. This is what makes Jesus such a compelling master and Lord to me. He never asks me to do one more thing than he was willing to do himself.

> To deny oneself, to take up one's cross, and to follow;
> To move ourselves out of the way enough to take on the burdens of others;
> To lay ourselves down for the needs of others;
> To pour our life out incessantly for others.

Life is given to us not to save and to hoard, but to risk and to spend.

A heart-warming story from the Stanford University Medical Center speaks to the meaning of "cross" very well. The doctors there had discovered that a rare and life-threatening blood disease was slowly sapping a young girl's life away. They knew of only one remedy for this disease—a transfusion from her younger brother. Because the younger brother miraculously had recovered from this same life-threatening disease earlier in his life, his blood now had antibodies that could fight off this disease that was now draining the life of his big sister. The doctors sat down with both of the children and told them as gently and as clearly as they could what the reality was. Finally the doctors turned to the little boy. "Are you willing to give Lisa a transfusion from your body?" With a trembling voice, he said, "Yes, for Lisa I will do *anything*."

They put the two children side by side in separate hospital beds and hooked them up. As the transfusion was going on, the little boy could see the color return to the face of his sister. He could see the brightness return to her eyes and the smile begin to cross her face. But he could see himself in the mirror, too. As his sister's face brightened, he noticed that his own complexion was becoming quite pale, and his own smile weakened. As the doctors were taking the needle out at the end of the transfusion, the little boy turned to the doctor and said, "Doctor, when will I start to die?"

Sacrifice and suffering and self-denial and taking on the way of the cross.

For him, I would do anything.

This is the heart of the matter for us who take following our Lord Christ seriously. This Lent, may we have the wisdom to see this message, and by God's grace have the courage to live it out!

The Robins Are Back

MARK 2:1–12

When he returned to Capernaum after some days, it was reported that he was at home. So many gathered around that there was no longer room for them, not even in front of the door; and he was speaking the word to them. Then some people came, bringing to him a paralyzed man, carried by four of them. And when they could not bring him to Jesus because of the crowd, they removed the roof above him; and after having dug through it, they let down the mat on which the paralytic lay. When Jesus saw their faith, he said to the paralytic, "Son, your sins are forgiven." Now some of the scribes were sitting there, questioning in their hearts, "Why does this fellow speak in this way? It is blasphemy! Who can forgive sins but God alone?" At once Jesus perceived in his spirit that they were discussing these questions among themselves; and he said to them, "Why do you raise such questions in your hearts? Which is easier, to say to the paralytic, 'Your sins are forgiven,' or to say, 'Stand up and take your mat and walk'? But so that you may know that the Son of Man has authority on earth to forgive sins"—he said to the paralytic—"I say to you, stand up, take your mat and go to your home." And he stood up, and immediately took the mat and went out before all of them; so that they were all amazed and glorified God, saying, "We have never seen anything like this!"

*T*he robins are back!

I was sitting in my office the other day, looking out the window, and I was almost overwhelmed by what I saw. Everywhere I looked there was barrenness; everything was dull, and everything was gray. There was no sign of life to be seen. It was a cloudy, miserable sort of day, and much of what I had shared with folks that day was filled with pain. It was one of those days very heavy to bear.

As I was looking out the window, all of sudden into that space flew a flock of robins. I was amazed at what happened to me when I saw them. Now, I am a lover of the natural world, but this day that flock of robins did something to boost my spirit which I have a hard time defining even to myself. But it happened. Those robins suddenly reminded me that the dullness and barrenness and the lifelessness was not the last word!

This story that Mark tells us has the same effect on me today as those robins had on my spirit a couple of weeks ago. Every time I reflect on it, I find something in me boosted and lifted, no matter how barren or lifeless or dull or painful everything is in my line of vision. It's a wonderful story, and it must have been very popular in the early Christian community because Mark told it first. Then Matthew thought it was a good enough thing to repeat, so he wrote it. Then Luke followed suit several years later. So it must have been at the heart of the tradition of the early church.

It's a story that made a tremendous impact then and has the same possibility of making an impact on us now.

The robins are back…a sign that winter is leaving. For some of us this has been an awful winter. For some of us it has been a winter of our discontent. For some of us it has been a winter marked with frustration, fear, and failure. For some of us it has been a winter of guilt. For some of us it has been a winter of marriage. For some of us it has been a winter of divorce. For some of us it has been a winter of new birth; but for some of us it has been a winter of the death of dreams. But the robins are back, and the story of the paralyzed young man continues to be told.

It's a fascinating scene. Jesus was coming home and rumor spread like wildfire that he was back in town, trying to have a little retreat for himself in a secluded house. Everybody knew where he was, and the house filled up almost instantly. People were so desperate to have what he offered. Jesus was talking to them, and not only was the house packed to capacity, but people were spilling over onto the sidewalk and into the street so that nobody could even walk by.

A small group of people came in from out of town. In the middle of this group was a smaller group of four, each person holding the handle of a stretcher. On the stretcher was the absolutely motionless body of a young man who was totally paralyzed. You can imagine the frustration of this group, so desperately wanting to have Jesus' healing touch, but seeing that they couldn't even get through, much less maneuver a stretcher through that crowd. They finally got up close to the house but saw that it was impossible to get in. Rather than turn around and go away, they looked around the side of the house and saw a staircase, which many Palestinian houses had because the residents used the roofs of their houses as patio gardens. The houses were usually so small and cramped, and people needed to get away for a little peace and quiet now and then, and the roof provided that sort of sanctuary. These four people climbed the staircase to the roof. When they got there, they found what was usually the case with Palestinian roofs—they were all flat, no pitch. The houses were usually small and rectangular and across the walls of the house were strung five or six beams placed three or four feet apart. On those beams were placed lots of saplings and branches and brush, which were packed in tightly and woven together. Over the top of this mixture was smeared a thick layer of mud to keep the rain and wind out. Many times on top of the mud on people's roofs grew a very lush lawn. So when the young men climbed up there and got off the staircase, they found themselves in the middle of a patio, and they wondered what to do.

They could hear below them the commotion. They could hear Jesus preaching. They started to scratch away at the roof, push back the grass, and dig away the dirt, and separate the branches; then they saw what was going on down there. Jesus was totally surrounded by people who were desperate to hear, desperate to be healed, desperate to be changed.

When they looked down, they saw that they were right above him; you can imagine their surprise! Then they lowered the stretcher until it rested at Jesus' feet. What would happen here if somebody started scratching through this roof about now, in the midst of this sermon? We would clear out of here, wouldn't we, or somebody would go outside and pull that person down. But Jesus was unflappable. He forgot the crowd, and he turned his attention to the one on the floor before him. He looked beneath the paralyzed, withered body, and saw a need greater than the restoration of the man's physical health.

He surprised everybody by speaking so tenderly and so directly to him. Some translations use the word "child" as the first word of Jesus' address. Our translation uses the word "son." But it is a very tender, intimate, soft way of addressing this person who probably had had very few people even speak to him in his life.

But Jesus didn't say, "Your body is healed." What did he say? "Your sins are forgiven." Now why in the world would he make a comment like that to someone who was totally paralyzed, who just wanted to walk around like everybody else?

Jesus spoke of forgiveness because he knew that somehow in this young man's life his spirit had been strangled. Something had caused a guilt, which had shut off all of his life forces. We know that happens today. We know the power of guilt to disrupt and destroy health. And Jesus knew that. He didn't know the reason for the guilt, nor do we. Clinically or spiritually, there is no way to tell, but Jesus sensed looking into that man's eyes that what he needed was the gift of forgiveness. In that moment, in that man, there was a whole new sense of being loved, of being valued. Once his sin was forgiven, then Jesus did the second thing. He told him to get up. Nobody had ever told him that before. But he got up and he rolled up the stretcher and his blanket. And Jesus said, "Now go on home." And he went home an entirely new person, walking in a way he had never walked before, seeing himself in a new light. This man's faith and hope were born, and his whole life was healed and restored.

Here is where we come in. Regardless of what kind of winter has us in its grip, regardless of the power of guilt, regret, or grief, no matter what it is that seems to strangle the life of our spirit, the power of Jesus' healing touch is now as it was then. "Son, daughter, you're healed; now go on home a different way." That day faith and hope found an opening, which doubt and faintheartedness would never have guessed was there, and that same possibility is open to each of us now.

Isaiah has already proclaimed to us, "Do not remember the former things or consider the things of old; I am about to do a new thing. Now it springs forth. Do you perceive it?"

Remember: the robins are back!

Pieces of Clay

If we could take all of Jesus' sayings in this lesson (Mark 8:31–33) and distill them down to their essence, one question would come out: What in me needs to die in order that Christ may live in me? The answers to this question will be as varied as there are people in this church today. Does fear need to die in me in order for Christ to live in me? Does hatred need to die in me in order for Christ to live in me? Does suspicion? Self-pity? This is a pertinent question for each of us as we take our steps toward Jerusalem in our Lenten pilgrimage. What needs to die in me that Christ might live in me?

———

(JOHN 2:13–22) Jesus drives the moneychangers out of the temple and asks questions about why we worship. Søren Kierkegaard, a Danish theologian, says that people usually think worship is a time when they come in and perform before God, who is our audience. He said our understanding is backwards, that when we come into church, God is the actor, the initiator, and we are those who listen with a will to be changed by what we see and hear. When we come in to worship, do we listen to Holy Scripture as if it were written to us? It was and we should, but we don't. When we say "amen" at the end of the prayers, do we say that as though we had written each prayer ourselves? We should, but we don't. The prayers would mean more if the amens were fuller. When we come to receive Eucharist and hold up empty hands, do we see that as a special gift to us? It is, intended just for us. But we have so little of our hearts, minds, or souls in our worship that it barely means anything at all. It is no wonder we say, "Glad it didn't last too long today; I have paid my dues and I am out of here." Hard questions Jesus asks us. Why do we worship, and what happens when we do?

———

As we travel through this Lenten journey, let's get back to basics: almsgiving, prayer, and fasting. We will hold up before ourselves these three vital signs against which we can measure our spiritual health at this point in our lives. These basic questions are, "How much do we practice almsgiving or generosity in our daily relationships? How much do we practice dependence upon God and a constant expression of gratefulness? How willing are we to discipline ourselves to rid our lives of destructive behaviors and attitudes?"

———

St. Benedict tells us that true humility is simply a measure of the self that is taken without exaggerated approval or exaggerated guilt. Humility is the ability to know ourselves as God knows us. Humility, then, is the foundation for our relationship with God, our connectedness to others, our acceptance of ourselves, our way of using the goods of the earth, and even our way of walking through the world without arrogance, without domination, without scorn, without putdowns, without disdain, without self-centeredness. The more we know ourselves, the gentler we will be with others.

Eastertide

At Easter we celebrate the new creation we can become, as we see our souls resurrected to a higher plane of beauty, hope, and joy. This step in our spiritual journey is akin to the potter's application of glaze over the drab surface of the clay, which gives it an unexpected luster and color.

*E*ASTER PRAYER: Lord Jesus, risen from the dead, freed from the tomb, come, we pray, and enter into our fear, doubt, and despair with the bright light of your presence. Help us to put our trust in you and in the power of your resurrection; that we may rejoice in you as our risen Lord and Savior, who lives and reigns with the Father and the Holy Spirit, one God, world without end. AMEN

Five Little Words

JOHN 20:1–18

Early on the first day of the week, while it was still dark, Mary Magdalene came to the tomb and saw that the stone had been removed from the tomb. So she ran and went to Simon Peter and the other disciple, the one whom Jesus loved, and said to them, "They have taken the Lord out of the tomb, and we do not know where they have laid him." Then Peter and the other disciple set out and went toward the tomb. The two were running together, but the other disciple outran Peter and reached the tomb first. He bent down to look in and saw the linen wrappings lying there, but he did not go in. Then Simon Peter came, following him, and went into the tomb. He saw the linen wrappings lying there, and the cloth that had been on Jesus' head, not lying with the linen wrappings but rolled up in a place by itself. Then the other disciple, who reached the tomb first, also went in, and he saw and believed; for as yet they did not understand the scripture, that he must rise from the dead. Then the disciples returned to their homes.

But Mary stood weeping outside the tomb. As she wept, she bent over to look into the tomb; and she saw two angels in white, sitting where the body of Jesus had been lying, one at the head and the other at the feet. They said to her, "Woman, why are you weeping?" She said to them, "They have taken away my Lord, and I do not know where they have laid him." When she had said this, she turned around and saw Jesus standing there, but she did not know that it was Jesus. Jesus said to her, "Woman, why are you weeping? Whom are you looking for?" Supposing him to be the gardener, she said to him, "Sir, if you have carried him away, tell me where you have laid him, and I will take him away." Jesus said to her, "Mary!" She turned and said to him in Hebrew, "Rabbouni!" (which means Teacher). Jesus said to her, "Do not hold on to me, because I have not yet ascended to the Father. But go to my brothers and say to them, 'I am ascending to my Father and your Father, to my God and your God.'" Mary Magdalene went and announced to the disciples, "I have seen the Lord"; and she told them that he had said these things to her.

*H*appy Easter! Jesus Christ was born for you. Jesus Christ lived for you. Jesus Christ suffered for you. Jesus Christ died for you. Jesus Christ was raised from the dead for you.

Now certainly all of those things are true for the entire creation—that Jesus was born for the world, Jesus lived for the world, Jesus suffered for the world, Jesus died for the world, and Jesus Christ was raised from the dead for the world.

But more importantly, as we celebrate this Easter moment, we need to remember that Jesus Christ was born; he lived; he suffered; he died, and he was raised for you.

It's hard for us to imagine today—in this marvelous place, surrounded by the sights and the smells of these lovely flowers—being uplifted by the "Alleluias" that we have said and sung; being cheered by this wonderful company of the faithful which we are a part of. It is hard for us to imagine, but the first Easter moment was exactly the *opposite* of everything we are experiencing right now.

It was not light and bright that first Easter; it was dark. John tells us this story of Easter through Mary Magdalene's own eyes. When Mary set out that morning on her long journey, it was dark. The text says very early, which means the last watch of the night—between 3:00 and 6:00 a.m. Mary was fumbling her way along in the dark all by herself. She wasn't going to the tomb to celebrate the resurrection of her Lord; she was going there to pay her last respects and to say her last good-bye. She wasn't going there to celebrate anything. She was going there to express the brokenness of her heart.

I can imagine what was running through Mary Magdalene's mind as she traveled that early morning. It might have been like a moment which occurred for her a couple of years before, a moment when she had walked up to Jesus as a tormented woman. Tradition has painted Mary Magdalene with a scarlet brush, but there is much over-dramatization of her sinfulness. We do know that Mary Magdalene presented herself to Jesus tormented and destroyed by seven demons; St. Luke tells us this. In that transforming moment, Jesus touched her life and gave her a whole new sense of direction, meaning, purpose, joy, and hope.

So she was probably going to Jesus' tomb to say, "Thank you, Lord, for turning my life upside down and inside out and totally around," because she probably hadn't thanked him enough when he was alive. Rather than going in the brightness and the lightness of it all, Mary Magdalene traveled in the dark, and rather than being surrounded by so great a cloud of witnesses, she traveled alone. She didn't go to that place with any sense of celebration—the way we feel at Easter. She went there to mourn, and she went there all by herself.

We face this Easter moment in our life—with all of the power and the promise of it—hoping that the same surprises which happened to Mary Magdalene will happen to us. If we are feeling as though we are wandering around in the darkness—that we are not quite sure where we are headed or what lies ahead—then Mary Magdalene can be our heroine. If we are besieged by doubts or disappointment or grief, Mary Magdalene can be our guide. If we have lost all hope in life, if we can't believe any improvement is possible, then Mary Magdalene can be our inspiration. What happened to her in her Easter moment can happen to us in this Easter moment in our own lives.

Mary Magdalene was the first to go to the tomb, and she was the last to leave the tomb. She was the first to proclaim an Easter sermon, and she set a pace that should be the pace for all preachers. She preached the shortest sermon ever preached on Easter, just five words—"I have seen the Lord." That's all it took. That's all it took to turn Mary's life around. She went back to tell the twelve, and their lives were turned around. A few months later this message reached five hundred, and their lives were turned around. That same message reaches our ears and our hearts and our minds now, and we hope to turn our lives inside out and upside down, too. We hope for a whole new purpose and a whole new direction for our living.

Clement of Alexandria had it right centuries ago when he

proclaimed, "The resurrected Christ turns all of our sunsets into dawn." *All of our sunsets into dawn!*

There is no grave so deep, there is no stone so large, and there are no grave bindings so strong that they cannot be overpowered by the same spiritual energy which was there in that resurrection moment centuries ago. The same spiritual energy is available to each of us now.

As we come to this time together with great joy and great celebration, a great sense of gratitude and a great awareness of beauty, let us come remembering that we, like Mary Magdalene, can be given *a whole new sense of life* this day—its importance, its meaning, its love, its grace, and its purpose.

My prayer for each of you is that you may lead the rest of your days according to this new beginning.

A Great Fish Story

JOHN 21:1–14

After these things Jesus showed himself again to the disciples by the Sea of Tiberias; and he showed himself in this way. Gathered there together were Simon Peter, Thomas called the Twin, Nathanael of Cana in Galilee, the sons of Zebedee, and two others of his disciples. Simon Peter said to them, "I am going fishing." They said to him, "We will go with you." They went out and got into the boat, but that night they caught nothing.

Just after daybreak, Jesus stood on the beach; but the disciples did not know that it was Jesus. Jesus said to them, "Children, you have no fish, have you?" They answered him, "No." He said to them, "Cast the net to the right side of the boat, and you will find some." So they cast it, and now they were not able to haul it in because there were so many fish. That disciple whom Jesus loved said to Peter, "It is the Lord!" When Simon Peter heard that it was the Lord, he put on some clothes, for he was naked, and jumped into the sea. But the other disciples came in the boat, dragging the net full of fish, for they were not far from the land, only about a hundred yards off.

When they had gone ashore, they saw a charcoal fire there, with fish on it, and bread. Jesus said to them, "Bring some of the fish that you have just caught." So Simon Peter went aboard and hauled the net ashore, full of large fish, a hundred fifty-three of them; and though there were so many, the net was not torn. Jesus said to them, "Come and have breakfast." Now none of the disciples dared to ask him, "Who are you?" because they knew it was the Lord. Jesus came and took the bread and gave it to them, and did the same with the fish. This was now the third time that Jesus appeared to the disciples after he was raised from the dead.

*I*t's a great story, this Easter story which John tells us! He was the only one who remembered and recorded it because he was the only one who would have been there. As an old man as he wrote down the Gospel, remembering this experience he had as a young man. And what an experience, what a story, it was!

The setting itself makes it a great story. It's sunrise at the beach. Who has not been moved by sunrise at the beach on a misty morning?

And there's a campfire. Whose heart is not warmed by the smell of driftwood and charcoal?

But probably what makes this such a wonderful story for me is that it is a great fish story. It turned out well for everybody involved, except maybe the fish, but it didn't really start out that way. At the beginning of the story, things are not right, and we can sense the frustration and failure of those people gathered there. It was early morning, and this group of people silently milled around in the boathouse wondering what to do, barely speaking to one another. They didn't really know what the next step was for them. It had been several weeks now since the Resurrection, and this tiny group of people had decided to leave Jerusalem in the south and head north, back to their home country.

So this band of seven went back home to Galilee, back to the same old place, the same old boats, the same old smelly nets, the same old fishing hole. Since they didn't know what to do next, they returned to the comfort of the familiar. They began to get back in touch with the water. These were true watermen, most of them. They made their living on the water, and they knew everything there was to know about it. But they were wondering what to do. Their community had been broken. We don't know where the other four disciples were. We don't really know why these seven had gathered themselves on that seashore that day. But there they were, fractured and isolated, uneasy with each other. They had lost the support, intimacy, and clarity they had just a month or so before. And here they were wandering around, scattered, confused, dazed, and not quite sure what to do next.

In his characteristic way, Simon Peter said, "I've had enough of this; I'm getting out of here, and I'm going fishing." He began to load up his boat with his nets; other people pulled their boats out of the boathouse and put them on the beach, and they began to push off. They entered the water late in the afternoon; the best fishing is at night since fish feed and school then. They fished all night long, and as the night was ending, they saw that this was just one of those nights. With empty nets and empty boats, they turned the bows of the boats toward the beach.

As they rowed, they began to notice through the mist coming off the water a figure walking up and down on the beach. They were slightly intrigued with that, but not very much, because they were looking down at their sore hands, probably very frustrated and disgruntled because they hadn't caught anything.

All of a sudden through the sea breeze they heard this voice, a voice which sounded slightly familiar, but a voice which spoke to them in an unfamiliar way. The speaker addressed them as children, and Jesus had never talked to them in that way before. But the certain clairvoyance, omniscience, and tenderness which they heard let them know who he was.

"You haven't caught anything, have you?" the voice asked.

The response was a pretty surly "no." Never ask a fisherman whether he has caught anything or not. It's embarrassing to admit that you haven't caught anything, especially when you make your living at it.

So they gave that surly response. Peter, suddenly with great insight, saw that it was his beloved Lord who was resurrected, standing there on the beach. Impetuous as he was, he jumped out of the boat and picked up his cloak on the way out. As a sign of respect, he knew he shouldn't meet his Lord wearing just his fishing shorts. He struggled to put on his cloak as he was running up the beach. When he got to the shore, sure enough, he found there his risen Lord.

The rest of the story gets even better! The rest of the story makes the Resurrection so real, so human, so realistic.

We tend to spiritualize the Resurrection so much that it loses touch with our daily life. But St. John reminds us in this fish story that the Resurrection occurs right in the midst of daily life. The disciples were not in the temple. They were not in some special place of meditation. They were doing what they had always done, the same old smelly business of fishing. And the resurrected Christ appeared to them right where they were.

This act on the part of Jesus was a pure gift of love to his friends. He knew of their bewilderment, their discouragement, their fatigue, their frustration, their failure, and their inadequacy. He came to them at this low point, right in the midst of life, to turn their lives around. All of a sudden they became empowered to become fishers of humankind, and not simply fishers of fish.

St. John noted there were 153 fish in that net. Now why would he be that particular about the number of fish? Jerome, an early church theologian, said that at that time there were 153 known varieties of fish, and consequently this specificity is John's way of saying that Jesus included everyone in his love. When that net was cast abroad, it was like the loving arms of Christ taking in all of creation, holding creation in his loving hands. John is saying that every one of us is included in the catch; not one of us is outside of it, excluded from it, no matter how seemingly isolated or alone.

With that catch that day, those early disciples realized that the resurrected presence of Christ would be with them always; this is where we all get in the boat with them. The Resurrection appears to us, too, in those moments when we are miserably discouraged. We have worked so hard; we have prayed so hard; we have hoped so hard for something; and we catch nothing. Nothing changes; nothing gets better; nothing heals; nothing clarifies.

It is at this moment—through the mist of the morning, in the midst of discouragement—that the power of the resurrected Christ takes hold and begins to cause us to look at ourselves and our mission in an entirely new light.

We are transformed!

Hope, which is crucified in us daily by despair, *arises*.

Reconciliation, which is crucified in us daily by alienation, *arises*.

Love, which is crucified in each of us daily by hatred, *arises*.

Truth, which is crucified in us daily by lies, *arises*.

Life becomes new by the virtue of the power of the resurrected Christ!

As day was breaking for those tired, disheartened disciples on that day long ago, they were welded back together with a new sense of purpose, which would propel them forward.

With his friends, Jesus was not only the loving, compassionate big brother. He was also a great fishing guide and a master chef—the greatest restorer of broken spirits and shattered dreams.

If we are willing to get in the boat with those disciples, this can be a new day for each of us as well. So expect it! Receive it! Go out of here and live it!

Mixed Emotions

LUKE 24:36–48

While they were talking about this, Jesus himself stood among them and said to them, "Peace be with you." They were startled and terrified, and thought that they were seeing a ghost. He said to them, "Why are you frightened, and why do doubts arise in your hearts? Look at my hands and my feet; see that it is I myself. Touch me and see; for a ghost does not have flesh and bones as you see that I have." And when he had said this, he showed them his hands and his feet. While in their joy they were disbelieving and still wondering, he said to them, "Have you anything here to eat?" They gave him a piece of broiled fish, and he took it and ate in their presence.

Then he said to them, "These are my words that I spoke to you while I was still with you—that everything written about me in the law of Moses, the prophets, and the psalms must be fulfilled." Then he opened their minds to understand the scriptures, and he said to them, "Thus it is written, that the Messiah is to suffer and to rise from the dead on the third day, and that repentance and forgiveness of sins is to be proclaimed in his name to all nations, beginning from Jerusalem. You are witnesses of these things."

They were so excited, and they were so enthusiastic. And yet at the same time they were very startled and they were terrified.

Now how could it be, that great mix of feelings in response to one human experience?

When St. Luke tells the story of the Resurrection he deals with the mystery of that experience in almost hushed tones, as though it is too profound or immense to describe. And yet he sets the scene perfectly for us. They were so excited and they were so enthusiastic because they were beginning to talk about experiences they had had of the risen presence of Christ. Everything had been revived about their spirits. These were people whose backs had been broken. They were huddled together in that upper room...all locked in. They were locked in because of fear. They were locked in not only physically because the door was locked, but they were locked in spiritually and emotionally because their fear had them so bound they did not even dare peek out the door. When they talked with one another, it was in hushed tones for fear of being recognized and also killed.

These were people who had had their hopes dashed and all of their dreams crushed. And yet they began to hear words that said the one whom they had followed for those three years was not dead, but was alive and was being experienced in life. But as they heard those words that caused their hearts to leap for joy, they also were startled by what they heard, and they were terrified by what it meant.

Translators use various words to translate the Greek that comes out in today's reading as startled. Some people use bewildered; some confused; some agitated; some frustrated; some upset; some troubled—all kinds of attempts at bringing this word into our understanding. But scripture says that these people were, in spite of their excitement and their enthusiasm, very perplexed by what they were hearing and were deeply troubled, almost terrified. These were people about to be kicked out of the nest. For three years they had enjoyed living in close proximity with Jesus day in and day out, and they had grown very safe and secure in the constant presence they had with him.

But they did not have that anymore; his death had taken that from them. In their grief and bewilderment, they were huddled up for fear, beginning to think about what uncertainty lay ahead. They knew that in the future they were not going to have the leadership or the guidance or the protection with which Jesus had sustained them in their discipleship. Now they were on their own. This was almost graduation day for the earliest apostles. It was their commencement into life, as they left behind everything which had given them meaning and security.

They could have stayed there in that room forever. The upper room could have become a prison in its safety. They could have stayed there out of nostalgia, remembering back on that last meal they had shared with their Lord. They could have thought about all the protection that those locked doors gave to them, but they knew that the proper time had come for them to be sent out, and they were startled and terrified.

I can understand how they felt. For most of life's great events we have mixed feelings, don't we? Very few experiences give us one pure feeling; usually there is a combination. We should not be startled by the fact that these earliest apostles had various feelings about this experience, too. Sure, they were excited about it; their hopes began to be revived. But they were also scared to death of what the implications might be for them. They were leaving the nest. And so when Jesus came into their midst just before they were kicked out, he came with two things: a gift and a mission.

The gift… what was the gift? Jesus said simply, "Peace be with you." Now in Jesus' day, the word "*Shalom*" was a greeting like "Hi, how are you?" Or "How are you doing?" Most people used it very flippantly, superficially, not really caring to stop for an answer. But Jesus gave this greeting as a gift to those people in the midst of the complexity of feelings which they were experiencing. Peace be with you.

What does he mean by peace? One thing I can say at the outset is what this peace is not. This is not peace of mind. We have so distorted the Gospel over the last twenty-five years to thinking that if we are faithful, we are going to be filled with peace of mind.

I would not be standing up here if peace of mind was a result of the faith to me, and I doubt that any of you would be here either. It is impossible to live with peace of mind…if we take life seriously. So many things crush me and agitate me. So many things happen in this life which dash my dreams and shatter my hopes, cause me fear. I would guess it is the same for each of you as well. That is the way life is for us! So Jesus' peace is not peace of mind. It is not the absence of conflict and pain. What did he do when he first stepped into the room? He exposed his wounds, his scars, to them. The resurrected Lord who brought the gift of peace is our scarred brother. The resurrected Lord is our battered leader. The resurrected Lord is our wounded healer. So peace is *not* the absence of conflict. Peace is not the absence of struggle and pain; we are going to have to face a variety of discomforting experiences in the midst of our life.

The peace that Jesus brought to those people was not the absence of anything, it was the presence: the presence of his love, the presence of his power, of his joy, of his hope, in the midst of the darkest circumstances of life. It was a presence from which nothing in all of creation could separate us.

This is the gift that he gave…the assurance that when you endure suffering, pain, conflict, grief, and fear, he would be by your side forever…the gift.

And then the mission. The mission then was not too clear, nor is it clear today. We wonder what it is that God's will has in store for us. How is it that we are to serve God? We think it was a lot easier then when those people had Jesus by their side to tell them directly. Well, he did not tell them directly what their mission was. We know about only two or three of those people huddled in that room. We know what happened to them; they became leaders of the church.

Most of them probably went back to their own professions, their own neighborhoods, their own homes, to their struggles, their heartbreaks, and their celebrations. But they went back there as transformed people because now they had a new sense of identity. This whole idea of identity crisis is not just an adolescent struggle. What in the world is God's will for my life in this circumstance or at this point? Each of us wonders. I am perplexed, confused, and not quite sure what our Lord Christ would have me do. This is a very normal, faithful, human, Christian struggle. So our Lord does not define for us what our mission is. None of us in this place is absolutely certain about what our specific mission in life is to be.

One of the things we know mission does not mean is that all of us should go out and begin the process toward holy orders. Mission does not have to do with ordination. Less than one percent of the church is ordained. The mission has to do with you and where you work and where you live, in your neighborhoods, in your homes. Are you there as a transformed person, knowing that the presence of our Lord Christ has made you different and demands that you be a different kind of person?

Early Christian people were called a third race; they were that different. No matter who they were, no matter where they went, no matter where they lived or what they did, they were a third race because their lives were transformed.

Now perhaps you're wondering, What does all this have to do with me? I want that gift of peace to be sure; I need this gift to comfort me, guide me, and cheer me. But what about the mission? What about me and the mission?

I wish I could define your mission for you, but I cannot. However, one person has helped me understand it a bit better. St. Francis came to a place in his life when he was kicked out of the comfortable and secure nest, and was transformed into a totally new way of being. And yes, he was afraid. The more seriously we take living the Christian life, the more afraid we are, too. Anybody who feels calm, easy, and good about that is not taking it seriously enough. But the mission which St. Francis describes for each of us is included in our Prayer Book. It is a wonderful prayer attributed to St. Francis (on page 833). Here is our mission. No matter who we are, where we work, where we live, what we do.

Lord, make us instruments of your peace. Where there is

hatred, let us sow love; where there is injury, pardon; where there is discord, union; where there is doubt, faith; where there is despair, hope; where there is darkness, light; where there is sadness, joy. Grant that we might not so much seek to be consoled as to console; to be understood as to understand; to be loved as to love. For it is in giving that we receive; it is in pardoning that we are pardoned; and it is in dying that we are born to eternal life.

That is our mission…an awesome challenge, day in and day out. It is crystal clear and it should scare us. It should perplex us, and it should bewilder us.

But as we make our next step together as Christ's people, our Lord Christ says to each of us this day, "My peace is my last gift to you."

All Locked Up

When it was evening on that day, the first day of the week, and the doors of the house where the disciples had met were locked for fear of the Jews, Jesus came and stood among them and said, "Peace be with you." After he said this, he showed them his hands and his side. Then the disciples rejoiced when they saw the Lord. Jesus said to them again, "Peace be with you. As the Father has sent me, so I send you." When he had said this, he breathed on them and said to them, "Receive the Holy Spirit. If you forgive the sins of any, they are forgiven them; if you retain the sins of any, they are retained." But Thomas (who was called the Twin), one of the twelve, was not with them when Jesus came. So the other disciples told him, "We have seen the Lord." But he said to them, "Unless I see the mark of the nails in his hands, and put my finger in the mark of the nails and my hand in his side, I will not believe." A week later his disciples were again in the house, and Thomas was with them. Although the doors were shut, Jesus came and stood among them and said, "Peace be with you." Then he said to Thomas, "Put your finger here and see my hands. Reach out your hand and put it in my side. Do not doubt but believe." Thomas answered him, "My Lord and my God!" Jesus said to him, "Have you believed because you have seen me? Blessed are those who have not seen and yet have come to believe." Now Jesus did many other signs in the presence of his disciples, which are not written in this book. But these are written so that you may come to believe that Jesus is the Messiah, the Son of God, and that through believing you may have life in his name.

What a thrilling evening that first Easter night turned out to be!

But it didn't start out that way. The evangelist John tells us that all during the weekend from the time of the Crucifixion to this time on Easter night, the remaining ten huddled together behind locked doors. They were not out proclaiming the Gospel from the rooftops, they were paralyzed by fear. They locked themselves away trying to have some peace of mind, some security, and some sense of safety.

Fear does that to us, doesn't it? It imprisons us. It locks us up and locks us away from so many of the joys and the beauties and the meanings of life. Fear cripples our spirits, crushes our hearts, dulls our minds, and keeps us from getting anywhere close to the good things in life which God wants us to have—especially the fear that accompanies grief.

Grief was a big part of what those people were feeling that first Easter night—plain and simple mourning. The one around whom they had built their lives for three years had been taken away. He had structured their life; he had guided them; he had inspired them; he had strengthened them; he had taught them. Now he was gone. The center of their life suddenly became a void because of the Master's death. The fear which gripped their hearts that evening took away all of their meaning, all of their purpose, and all of their security.

That's what grief does to us when it hits. We wonder if we can go on. We wonder if there is any purpose. We wonder where the structure is. We wonder if there is going to be any joy in life again. This fear tends to lock us up inside of ourselves so that we really cease to live. This was one of the fears that gripped those ten for that weekend—the fear caused by their mourning—but I think there was another level of fear as well. They had heard how excruciating crucifixion was as a way to die. They knew that it was the most painful method of execution known to mankind. Because they were somehow allied with Jesus during their life, they were locked behind those closed doors; they were sure that at any moment the Roman soldiers were going to knock, push that door open, slam them against the wall, drag them through the streets, and hang them on their own crosses. They were afraid of the costliness of the commitment, which they had made to Jesus as their Lord. They were afraid they were going to have to suffer the same fate he had faced.

We would have probably been locked up, too, if we had been in their shoes. It is very easy to judge these people, to say it's a shame that they didn't pass the test. I feel certain that we would be huddled up together in a locked room somewhere, too. They were in the upper room most likely. This was the place where they had spent that last wonderful evening with their Lord in their last intimate meal together, where everything had been peaceful and secure and comfortable. And here they were now, locked up in the same place, which was now anything but comfortable and peaceful—a place of torment and a place of terror. There might have been another reason those disciples were afraid, probably the greatest reason of them all. You remember that Mary Magdalene and Peter and John had come back to them on Sunday morning, telling them that Jesus was not in the tomb. Remember how they said that Jesus was raised from the dead and that the tomb no longer held him and that he was going to be alive in the world? The disciples were afraid of what it might be like to confront his presence. In their heart of hearts they knew that when Jesus was about to be crucified, they all abandoned him. Every one of them chickened out and fled.

Jesus had asked a couple of them to pray with him for a while that last evening of his own life while he struggled with his own dying. They couldn't; they slept. He asked them to be with him at the cross; they weren't. No one knows where they were. Gutless wonders, they were, cowards all. I can imagine as they anticipated seeing their Lord again, they dreaded what he was going to say to them. We know how it is when we let folks down, don't we? We wonder how they are going to confront us the next time. We wonder what they are going to say. They expected to see Jesus' long skinny finger of judgment pointed squarely between their eyes. "Where were you when I needed you? Where were you when you said you would go with me to my death? I didn't see any of you in the crowd that day? Where was your courage? Where was your commitment?"

Their own guilt had them locked up behind those closed doors. But lo and behold, what happened? John doesn't tell us about the mystery of how Jesus entered through the locked door. John simply says that Jesus is there. He appeared. But instead of making his disciples feel worse, instead of pounding on them the way they expected, he offered them something entirely different. They deserved the worst. Jesus, the risen

Christ, gave them the best. Instead of more torment and more pain, he simply opened wide his hands and said, "My peace I give to you. My peace is my gift to you."

He had to say this twice. It took a double dose because their fear and their guilt were that strong. But when Jesus spoke, he wasn't simply giving that casual Eastern greeting, *"Shalom."* Everybody sort of nodded and said *"Shalom"* back then—similar to our saying, "Hi, how are you?"—not stopping to hear the answer. But Jesus said, "Here. Here is my peace." When Jesus said that, he was not simply saying, "I'm giving you serenity or I'm giving you calm or I'm giving you some comfort." In Hebrew, that word means "May God give you every good thing." What a difference that is. Instead of the judgment they expected, instead of the criticism they deserved, instead of the harsh confrontation they thought was coming, Jesus held out his scarred hands and said, "I have a gift for you." Instead of tormenting them, he said, "I pray that God will give you every good thing." And he didn't stop there. In his own mind, he was probably thinking, "I know you've let me down; I know you ran away; I know you are weak; I know you are selfish; I know you get afraid easily; I know your commitment is flimsy. But I am going to entrust to you the care of this Gospel because I can't spread it to the entire world. I need you to take this good news to the darkness and the pain and the despair of the world around you."

What a surprise that must have been! These people who couldn't come through in a pinch all of a sudden were reinvested with another responsibility. Jesus said, "I'm going to try you again because I have confidence that you can be the bearers of this good news to a hurting and needful world."

What a surprise it must have been as they began to look at themselves anew and to think, "Can he trust me again? Can I come through this time? Do I have what it takes?"

Since the answer was no, Jesus gave them another gift. "I will give you my spiritual energy," he said. "You are not in this by yourself because I know you can't do it alone. So rather than agonize about this truth, take from me the spiritual energy and power which can enable you to be Easter people."

So we sit here with our fears, with our guilt, with our flimsy commitments, with our responsibilities undertaken and unfulfilled. We sit here with our own sinfulness ever before us, and we hear once again those words, "To you I entrust my Gospel; and if my Gospel is to make any impact on the world, it is *you* who must make the impact."

Wow! What a surprise! What a gift! As we hear this post-Easter message once again, we can join those ten people locked in that room. We can burst the doors of this place wide open and can open our hearts and minds. We can receive our Lord's power, and we can become once again not only the people of the Advent, but Christ's Easter people. By God's grace, may that be so.

Breaking the News

LUKE 24:1–10

But on the first day of the week, at early dawn, they came to the tomb, taking the spices that they had prepared. They found the stone rolled away from the tomb, but when they went in, they did not find the body. While they were perplexed about this, suddenly two men in dazzling clothes stood beside them. The women were terrified and bowed their faces to the ground, but the men said to them, "Why do you look for the living among the dead? He is not here, but has risen. Remember how he told you, while he was still in Galilee, that the Son of Man must be handed over to sinners, and be crucified, and on the third day rise again." Then they remembered his words, and returning from the tomb, they told all this to the eleven and to all the rest. Now it was Mary Magdalene, Joanna, Mary the mother of James, and the other women with them who told this to the apostles.

Happy Easter! I am overcome every year when we share this greeting, overcome for several reasons. First of all I am astounded by the power of this great expression of the heart of the faith, which draws us together today. But I am also overcome because I find this to be the toughest of all days to preach. I always face this day with more trepidation than other days because of the inadequacy I feel about plumbing the depths of the mystery of the Resurrection. I worry that whatever I say might trivialize or miss the point of the power of this momentous experience. And yet we will persevere in spite of my worry and intimidation.

This year throughout Lent I have reflected many times on the Gospel we share today. One word recurred in my meditation that seemed to leap out of this Gospel account time and again. The word was "breaking." The word "breaking" gives us a framework for our reflection on the mystery of Easter. First of all, there is the breaking of a new day, the time when shards of light begin to pierce the deep darkness of the night. A new day. A new day can cause both foreboding and anticipation. At the breaking of a new day those women were going to the tomb that first Easter morn in the fogginess of a gray day filled with sadness and uncertain about what the day would bring. Now we move to the second aspect of breaking, their breaking hearts. Those women were not on a joyful journey that morning. They were going to the grave loaded down with all the spices they needed to anoint the body of their beloved Lord in preparation for burial. So they made their way through the breaking of the day with breaking, heavy hearts. Suddenly they encountered the breaking open of the tomb, which astounded them and paralyzed them with fear.

Mark's Gospel account relates the conversation those women shared on the way to the tomb that morning, a conversation focused on the anxiety they felt about the huge boulder which had been pushed up to the door of the cave in which Jesus' body had been placed. The women were worried that they would not be able to move the boulder out of the way and would not be able to fulfill their mission. But they were amazed to discover that the power of God had broken open the tomb by moving aside the huge boulder.

When they went inside the cave, there was the exciting breaking of news to them. The two figures who greeted them in the empty tomb gave them a message of hope to take back to the disheartened and despairing disciples who had abandoned their Lord. The breaking news announced a new reality, which would empower those people to become persons they never imagined they could become.

So here we have the framework of the Resurrection experience. The breaking of a new day. Perhaps some of us stand on the threshold of a day we may be facing with foreboding or anticipation. If that is so for you, the experience of the Resurrection can give you hope. The breaking of our hearts. Some of us face this day with hearts filled with sadness and need to sense the joy which the Resurrection can bring. Remember, those women went to that empty tomb with hearts burdened by grief. So if that is where you are today, if you come to this empty moment with a heart broken by grief, the Resurrection experience can enable you to carry on. A wise friend of mine whose heart was broken by mourning told me one day that loss makes artists out of all of us as it forces us to reweave the fabric of our lives.

That is what was happening to those women that morning. When they saw that the tomb had been broken open, they discovered new possibilities of life and hope which they would have never thought possible. When they went to the grave, they did not find death. Instead they confronted the announcement: the breaking news of a whole new way of life that was offered to them and to the whole world. They broke this news to the disciples, whose lives also were broken open to a whole new reality. The power of the Resurrection turned their lives upside down and inside out, and their witness to the promise of new life they had been given transformed the life of the world around them.

The Resurrection is not merely a past experience which we remember this day, my friends. It is an occurrence that we celebrate at this very moment in our life. Resurrection is a force, a principle. It is life's gravity. Resurrection is a dynamic of God's new life held out to all of us all the time.

I was fascinated by one phrase in the Gospel. When the good news was broken, where was it to be found? In Galilee, say the messengers. Now when Galilee is mentioned, it is not a reference to a little geographical pinpoint in the Middle East. Galilee represents all of life, right down to this present time. Galilee is where people work and people play. Galilee is where babies are born and people grow old. Galilee is where people marry and where people divorce. Galilee is where people succeed and where people fail. Galilee is where people live in peace and people live in fear. And Galilee is where people are lonely and people live in security. Galilee is Spartanburg. Galilee is the Church of the Advent. And the Resurrection is just as possible for each one of us here today as it was for those women who went with breaking hearts at the break of day to that broken-open tomb to receive the good news, broken to them that there was new life possible beyond the death and defeat of Good Friday.

So we see that the heart of the Easter message is profoundly simple. Hope is the heart of the message. If only we could marinate our spirits in that hope for the fifty days of Eastertide, there is no telling what Christ's resurrected presence could do with us as individuals or as a community of faith. No matter where we are in our life's journey, no matter how dark our night, no matter how heavy our boulder, no matter how overwhelming our defeat, no matter how crippling our loneliness, God holds out to each of us a promise of new life that we cannot even begin to anticipate on our own.

And then there is that final breaking: Jesus' promise that he would meet his followers in the breaking of the bread. This is what draws us together this day: our Lord's broken body given to each of us. As we gather in faith and hope, he feeds, he nourishes, he strengthens, he guides, and he gives the possibility of new life to us, one and all. It is only because of his presence that we can say to one another this day, Happy Easter!

Pieces of Clay

As God's Easter people we are called to look at life from the side of the living and not of the dead. This is very difficult and quite a challenge while we are surrounded by much darkness, fear, and heaviness in life. Our task is to become aware that we are surrounded by the Resurrection at every moment, this moment and all others. But sometimes we are like the little bird who is always asking her mother, "Where is the sky?" unaware that the sky is the very place in which she flies. Eastertide ebbs and flows, but it always surrounds us with its power and its promise of new life ahead.

—

Easter, 2003. Each of us brings our own set of anxieties to this moment as we stand in the midst of war once again. We have many uncertainties, not only about the present, but the aftermath, the horror of what might come, and the wondering about the cause of it all. We wonder what lies ahead. Who is going to push that great stone of anxiety which blocks the opening in our lives? Who will remove the fear, which can cripple us and close us off from the future God has in store for us? Perhaps the great stone rolled up against your life is not simply fear. Maybe it is disillusionment, hopelessness, or an overpowering sense of grief. The great stone might be called guilt, guilt about something we have either done or left undone, which is crippling us in our own sense of failure. Maybe it is a sense of foreboding about our own aging and the limitations we will face. But, lo and behold, when the women reached the tomb they discovered that somehow, in the mystery of it all, the power of God had pushed away the great stone and they found, instead of death, an empty space full of possibilities of new life. This is part of this great celebration of Easter. The mystery that was theirs can be ours today.

Pentecost

During Pentecost we begin to discover how we can develop into the persons God created us to be as we follow the example of life he has shown to us in the resurrected presence of his Son, our Lord Jesus Christ. This stage in the pottery process represents the usefulness of the pot as it becomes the beautiful vase, vessel, or receptacle it was envisioned to be by the potter.

PRAYER FOR PENTECOST: Gracious and generous God, giver of all things: Take our eyes and see through them. Take our mouths and speak through them. Take our hands and serve through them. Take our hearts and set them on fire for you, your Gospel, and your world through the grace and power of the one who came to show us how, your Son, Jesus our Lord. AMEN

May I Light Your Lamp?

JOHN 14:8–17

Philip said to him, "Lord, show us the Father, and we will be satisfied." Jesus said to him, "Have I been with you all this time, Philip, and you still do not know me? Whoever has seen me has seen the Father. How can you say, 'Show us the Father'? Do you not believe that I am in the Father and the Father is in me? The words that I say to you I do not speak on my own; but the Father who dwells in me does his works. Believe me that I am in the Father and the Father is in me; but if you do not, believe me because of the works themselves. Very truly, I tell you, the one who believes in me will also do the works that I do and, in fact, will do greater works than these, because I am going to the Father. I will do whatever you ask in my name, so that the Father may be glorified in the Son. If in my name you ask me for anything, I will do it. If you love me, you will keep my commandments. And I will ask the Father, and he will give you another Advocate, to be with you forever. This is the Spirit of truth, whom the world cannot receive, because it neither sees him nor knows him. You know him, because he abides with you, and he will be in you."

Jesus said, "If you love me, you will keep my commandments." The greatest contribution our Lord Christ made to religious thought was his taking the hundreds of regulations, laws, and commandments which his people had lived by for centuries and distilling all of them into one—the commandment to love. Previously Jesus had said to his followers, "You've heard in your past that there are numerous regulations regarding practices you should and should not do; but I say to you that the summary of all of these is to love." To love God first, to love others, then to be able to love ourselves as well. So in this incident, when he says, "If you love me you will do my commandment," Jesus is reminding us of his great commandment that above all we are to be people who love.

It seems almost a contradiction in terms that we be commanded to love. But he did command us for two reasons. First, because it is very difficult to love, and secondly because each of us desperately needs to know that we are loved. It is the one thing in life that we cannot do without. We can be well fed and well clothed; we can have all of the symbols of success and security; but if we do not know that we are loved, then our souls and our spirits shrivel. Our Lord knows how desperately each of us needs to love and be loved for our spiritual, emotional, and physical health. On the other hand we are commanded to love because it is not our human nature to do so.

We are told by depth psychologists that our first instinct is to meet our own needs and to protect ourselves. So when Jesus commands us to love he is asking us to work against our nature; he is asking us to do what is so difficult—to love, to set the needs of others above our own. And when Jesus speaks about love in this instance, he is not referring to anything sentimental; he is not talking about warmth or affection or anything romantic. Jesus is talking not about matters of the heart but matters of the will. To love is not a certain way of feeling, but a certain way of behaving. But it is difficult to behave in loving ways, to set the needs of others before our own. Think how our marriages would be transformed by this type of love; what a difference this type of loving behavior could bring between parents and children. Think what a dynamic impact this would make on the places where we work and where we play. To love is to act. It is a decision to set the needs of others above our own.

Mother Teresa was a person who exemplified this way of life. She made a decision early in her life to set aside her own needs and to focus entirely on the needs of those beyond her. We all know something of the grand works of loving sacrifice that she performed. She wrote a book called *One Heart Full of Love,* which sums up the reasons she lived her life in obedience and faithfulness. In that book she tells stories about the ways God worked through her to love people into life.

One account that is particularly touching to me came out of the establishment of a new home for her sisters in Australia. This home was located close to a tribe of aboriginal people who lived in squalid conditions we cannot even imagine. As was her custom whenever a new home was opened, Mother Teresa would go there and live for awhile so she could help the sisters get established and become acquainted with the people in the communities they were to serve.

As she walked about this tiny village day after day, she noticed an old man sitting outside a deplorable hut with his head down, never looking up, day and night sitting there with his eyes to the ground. She would speak every time she passed him but never got a response. Then one day she decided to stop to talk to this old man. She knelt down in front of him and began to ask him some questions about his life. He would not look up but he would shake his head yes or no. Finally she said almost in desperation, "May I clean up your house? May I make your bed?"

Reluctant at first, he finally agreed. She stepped inside his dark and dingy hut and found it even worse inside than it looked from the outside. She could barely see because there were only slits in the walls through which slivers of light shone. But as she began to poke around in the midst of all the mess and the clutter, she saw in the corner a lamp. She could tell right away that it was a very fine lamp but it was covered with cobwebs, filth, and dust. She did not mention it right away but went about cleaning up a bit and throwing out some trash. As she worked she began to talk more with the old gentleman and finally she dared to ask him about his lamp. She said, "The lamp there, do you ever light it?" He said, "Why? Why would I ever need to light my lamp? I would only light that lamp if someone came to visit me. No one ever comes to see me, so for years that lamp has not been lit."

Touched almost to tears, Mother Teresa continued tidying up the place and finally asked him, "If my sisters came by to see you everyday, would you light the lamp for them?" Reluctantly he replied, "I will think about it." So she went back to the home, gathered the sisters around her and told them about this elderly man and assigned one of them to go by and visit him at dusk every day, which she did. Gradually when the nun appeared she would see the lamp shining through the slits in the wall. One day the man said to the sister, "Go and tell your friend that when she came to see me, she lit the lamp of love in my life, and it has burned ever since."

It seemed like a small thing, but in that dark and desperate loneliness the lighting of that lamp was a symbol that this man had been loved into being because someone had dared to care and to help. The visits continued for two years until one night that old man died, in a very tidy house, in a crisp clean bed with a sparkling lamp brightly shining beside him.

Jesus said, "I'm going away but I'm going to leave you here to do greater things than I have ever done." This is a frightful thought to me; maybe it is to you. Jesus knew it would be impossible for us to become people who loved in his dynamic, transforming way, if we were left to our own resources. And so he said, "I'm not going to leave you alone; I'm going to send you another, one who would be a helper, strengthener, and guide," one whom scripture translates as an *advocate*.

The word "advocate" really means "one who is called in to stand beside." So we are not in this alone, my friends, as we face this commandment together today. We are called to be people who love, people who are willing to go beyond our own needs to extend ourselves to the needs of others. And in so doing, we are to be people who are sent into life to transform it, to help light lamps, and to help love people into being.

This is what Pentecost is all about. Those tongues of fire were splinters of God's love going into each participant. Those tongues of love empowered them to move beyond their fears, beyond their own self-seeking, into a commitment to be obedient and generous beyond imagining. So on Pentecost once again we celebrate this festival of love. Our Moravian brothers and sisters call the Eucharist a love feast, and that it is! We celebrate the outpouring of God's love to us. We take it into ourselves and we become people who are then empowered to make a decision, a decision to be people who are sent to love others into life.

*F*irst Impressions

LUKE 9:18–24

Once when Jesus was praying alone, with only the disciples near him, he asked them, "Who do the crowds say that I am?" They answered, "John the Baptist; but others, Elijah; and still others, that one of the ancient prophets has arisen." He said to them, "But who do you say that I am?" Peter answered, "The Messiah of God."

He sternly ordered and commanded them not to tell anyone, saying, "The Son of Man must undergo great suffering, and be rejected by the elders, chief priests, and scribes, and be killed, and on the third day be raised."

Then he said to them all, "If any want to become my followers, let them deny themselves and take up their cross daily and follow me. For those who want to save their life will lose it, and those who lose their life for my sake will save it…"

*T*hroughout my life, as I have reflected on Holy Scripture, I have discovered that my spiritual growth is enhanced far more by the questions it raises than by the answers it gives. I don't know whether or not this is true for you, but my faith is always challenged, my spirit stretched, and my understanding of life deepened as I face into the questions that scripture holds up before me. I believe it was the same way for our Lord.

Jesus was a master teacher. We notice all through the Gospels that whenever someone approached Jesus wanting a simple answer to a very complicated situation, instead of giving a direct answer, he usually told them a perplexing story. He rarely answered questions directly, because he wanted people to struggle continually in their growth in faith, and he knew this growth would be nurtured more by personal inquiry than by accepting answers from others. This is exactly what is related in the Gospel incident this morning.

We need to set the stage a little bit. Jesus has been about his public ministry for a couple of years now. In that period of time he has created quite a stir in his homeland. He has performed some amazing works. He has taught some wonderful lessons. He has built some magnificent communities among strangers. So he has created quite a bit of notoriety for himself. He is aware that he has created a variety of ardent supporters as well as an equal number of violent opponents. So when we reflect on Jesus' life through this part of the Gospel for today, we find him struggling by himself in prayer, trying to sort it all out. He is just about to turn his face to Jerusalem and go toward his suffering and his death, his moment of great decision. Here he is at this turning point in his life. We don't know what he is praying about but we can assume he was struggling because of the question that comes out of his prayer.

Jesus was wondering what the word on the street was about him. Since he didn't get around as much as the disciples whom he had sent out to the far reaches of their world, Jesus wanted to gather them up and try to learn what impression he was making on other people. I can imagine that he was bewildered by what he heard. One disciple reported that someone said, "You sound like John the Baptist. You look a little different but your message is the same. Maybe you are John the Baptist who has come back to us to repeat the message of repentance." Another disciple said he heard, "No, he's not John the Baptist at all. He's that old prophet Elijah. He has that same kind of fiery spirit. Surely he's Elijah." Other people said, "No, he's much older than that. He represents the best of our prophetic tradition."

So the disciples must have been confused as they heard one another talk about how Jesus was being perceived by the world. And Jesus himself was even more perplexed. So he responded, "It really does matter that much what people are saying." He probably was aware that we always make many different impressions on other people. This is an insight that we need to take seriously today: the influence we have on other people around us, the effect we create, the impressions we make.

We know we are going to make a variety of impressions on other people. Some impressions are more accurate than others, but no one will ever know us exactly as we know ourselves, no matter how hard we try to impress. The important thing Jesus was saying is that we should strive to have integrity in this life so that what people see of us on the outside is a true reflection of what is on the inside. He encourages us to be honest with ourselves in our interaction with others so that people will perceive us as the true selves that God has created us to be.

Then Jesus turned the question on those who were his closest friends. He said, "I don't really care what the world says. I really care what you say. You are the most important people in the world to me. Who do you say that I am?" I can imagine that eyes were downcast, and feet were shuffling in response to his question. Impetuous old Peter blurted out, "I know who you are,

Jesus. You are the Messiah of God." Jesus immediately hushed him up because he knew "Messiah" was a dangerous word which conjured up an image of a person like General Patton. The Jewish faithful thought the Messiah was going to come as a powerful military figure to throw off foreign oppression and to restore liberty to the land of Israel. So Jesus said, "Don't use that word because you don't yet understand what it means to be the Christ of God." Then Jesus continued to explain that his way of being was grounded in sacrificial self-giving. Jesus declared that he would be known as "The Man for Others." And this is his expectation for each of us.

Whether we like it or not every one of us is a follower. Some of us are very independent and pride ourselves on our autonomy, our own way of thinking and behaving. There is probably a bit of that characteristic in all of us. All of us should acknowledge that we are followers of something if we are honest with ourselves. Some of us might even be chasing something. Here Jesus asks us what we are following in this life. Is it status we have to achieve? Is it a certain lifestyle we are driven to create? Is it success or notoriety in the world? What gets us up in the morning and drives us through the day? Jesus asks us further, "Is what you are following giving you the fulfillment and joy which God intends for you to have in your life?"

Thomas Merton, one of my favorite theological philosophers, said to one of his students, "If you really want to know who I am, don't ask me where I live, or how I make my living, or what I like to eat, or what my favorite hobbies are. If you really want to know who I am, ask me what I am living for and really push me on that. And then when I try to answer this question, ask me another. Ask me what it is that keeps me from living into what I want to live for." Unsettling questions, but the answers lead us deeper and deeper into truth.

I have discovered a book recently that has become a real serendipity to me. It has an intriguing title, *How to Think Like Leonardo DaVinci*, by Thomas Gelb. This book has been transforming for me because it has helped me sharpen the questions of my life as I go on into my future. One of the fascinating things to me about Leonardo is that his journal has hundreds of pages of nothing but questions. I love that. He answers one question with another question, and with each question he digs deeper into what is true about this life and how we are called to live it. Leonardo was never satisfied with what he created. He left many projects unfinished because he was constantly striving to discover the next level of truth or creativity.

This morning Jesus asks us the same question he asked his closest friends back then, "Who do you say that I am? If you are serious about following me, what difference does it make in the way you are living your life on a daily basis?" When Jesus refers to picking up your cross, he is not talking about martyrdom. Jesus is talking about a daily taking up of one's cross and realizing the powerful influence we have on people who may be following us. This can be an unsettling realization for those of us who are fathers. What influence are we having on those who live with us in that most intimate of circles? How aware are we of the power we have over others? It is here that Jesus reminds us that there is only one way to realize joy and fulfillment, and that is to live the way of sacrificial self-giving. We must become willing to place the needs of others above our own.

Another of my favorite Roman Catholic theologians was a priest, physicist, philosopher, and poet named Teilhard de Chardin. He wrote a profound book called *The Phenomenon of Man* in which he said, "For you there is only one road that can lead to God and that is fidelity. To remain constantly true to yourself, to what you feel is highest in you. The road will open before you as you go. Do not forget that the value and interest of life is not so much to do conspicuous things as to do the ordinary things with the perception of their enormous value." To do the ordinary things day by day with the perception of their enormous value…this is the essence of following Christ into the joyful, abundant way of life. The way is given to each of us. Who do we say that he is, and what does our answer have to do with the way we live? Questions which will take us the rest of our lives to answer.

As Sheep Among Wolves

MATTHEW 10:16–33

Jesus said to the twelve apostles, "See, I am sending you out like sheep into the midst of wolves; so be wise as serpents and innocent as doves. Beware of them, for they will hand you over to councils and flog you in their synagogues; and you will be dragged before governors and kings because of me, as a testimony to them and the Gentiles. When they hand you over, do not worry about how you are to speak or what you are to say; for what you are to say will be given to you at that time; for it is not you who speak, but the Spirit of your Father speaking through you. Brother will betray brother to death, and a father his child, and children will rise against parents and have them put to death; and you will be hated by all because of my name. But the one who endures to the end will be saved. When they persecute you in one town, flee to the next; for truly I tell you, you will not have gone through all the towns of Israel before the Son of Man comes.

"A disciple is not above the teacher, nor a slave above the master; it is enough for the disciple to be like the teacher, and the slave like the master. If they have called the master of the house Beelzebub, how much more will they malign those of his household! So have no fear of them; for nothing is covered up that will not be uncovered, and nothing secret that will not become known. What I say to you in the dark, tell in the light; and what you hear whispered, proclaim from the housetops. Do not fear those who kill the body but cannot kill the soul; rather fear him who can destroy both soul and body in hell. Are not two sparrows sold for a penny? Yet not one of them will fall to the ground apart from your Father. And even the hairs of your head are all counted. So do not be afraid; you are of more value than many sparrows.

"Everyone therefore who acknowledges me before others, I also will acknowledge before my Father in heaven; but whoever denies me before others, I also will deny before my Father in heaven."

*L*ife is difficult. So says Scott Peck in the opening sentence of his widely acclaimed book, *The Road Less Traveled.* This short, yet truthful and powerful, sentence written about twenty years ago, is the kernel from which everything else grows—as Dr. Peck describes—the magnitude of responses we can make to the challenges of living. The Christian life is even more difficult to live, says our Lord Christ to his followers just before he kicks them out of the nest. They have been huddled behind him for about eighteen months and have followed him like a school of fish everywhere he went. They have watched and listened. They have been puzzled and they have been empowered, and all of a sudden it is their turn to step up.

Jesus is saying, "I'm stepping aside now and I'm sending you out there. You are to go in my stead and to do those things I have done, to say those things I have said. You are now going in my place." Then Jesus becomes realistic. There is nothing idealistic at all about Jesus, and the more I get to know him, the more I am impressed by his ability to face right into the hard truths of life.

Scott Peck does offer valid insight when he tells us that life is difficult and that we should expect it to be no other way. If we then dare to take on a Christian way of living, life is going to be even more difficult for us than it is otherwise. Here Jesus used an almost harsh metaphor to make a point with his closest friends. He said, "I'm sending you out there now as sheep among wolves." In this instance, I can imagine Jesus' heart was heavy as he told them this because he would have liked to cheer them up with a rousing pep talk and send them out hollering into the field. Instead he referred to them as sheep among wolves. That's a harsh metaphor, isn't it? Sheep among wolves. "The world is going to do everything it can to resist and undermine you, so be aware that there will be strongly negative, even life-threatening, responses to you if you are true to what I tell you."

As I envision this talk Jesus is giving his varsity squad, it is like he is in the locker room with them, getting them ready for the biggest game of their life. He is wanting to let them know what they are going to face when they leave the safety and security of that place. Now, if I had been on his team, if I had been playing ball for Jesus at that time and heard his talk, I would have probably taken off my uniform before I even hit the field. I think most of us would be tempted to abandon the team because what we hear is not easy to hear, truthful though it is.

So Jesus was saying, "If you take on the seriousness of the Christian life don't expect to be immune to reactions that are going to hurt you, or maybe threaten your life. Yet I want you to go out there and be true to this mission I give you. I want you to go out there and be as sheep among wolves." Then he mixes metaphors and uses another image as he says, "I want you to be as wise as serpents, but I want you to be as harmless and innocent as doves."

Now how in the world do we put those two together? There are people in this life who are out to get us, people who will wish us harm, people whom we threaten, people whom we anger, people who simply are going to respond to us in negative, threatening ways. Life is like that, and we shouldn't expect any immunity. But Jesus didn't tell us to be paranoid about every person we meet as a potential life-threatening force; however, he did say to be realistic about our life. There are going to be many people out there who want to undo all of the good that we have tried to do. Jesus warned, "When you go out there, I want you to be smart; I don't want you to be foolish. I want you to be aware of the evil, which is going to hurt your body and your soul. But I want you to venture out nevertheless, and when you do, I want you to be gentle, tender, and compassionate."

Here is probably the toughest challenge of all. It's easy to be suspicious, isn't it, and to avoid people we fear may do us harm. It is so tough to enter into life aware of the hurts which await us. It is even more difficult to face this pain without returning hurt for hurt, vengeance for vengeance, to be harmless and innocent instead.

This is a tough way to live. Life is difficult enough on its own it seems, and I wish Jesus would give us a better pep talk as he sends us out into the world. But Jesus, being the realist that he is, knows what we must face. So the first part of this Gospel is discomforting and disquieting to me as I take it in for myself. I wish it were different. But the second part of the

Gospel, if we get the full truth here, offers us comfort to balance the discomfort. Jesus begins to talk about the intimacy of God with his children. Regardless of our best efforts in our earthly families, Jesus says clearly that sometimes brothers are going to be pitted against brothers, and children against parents, and parents against children. Sometimes there will be alienation and divisions that are final and absolute. When you find yourself in one of these situations, painful though it is, know that your heavenly Father is there with you.

Jesus then uses a couple of other images which are very comforting. He calls our attention to a sparrow, since he is probably looking at a little flock of birds hopping around. Sparrows were the cheapest sacrifice that Jewish people could offer to God. You could get more sparrows for a penny than any other creature alive. They were the cheapest of all, having the least value. Yet Jesus says, "There is not a sparrow in creation which is outside the scope of your heavenly Father's awareness and care, and you have much more value than any sparrow."

Often a faith crisis occurs for us when life is too difficult… sometimes life is too difficult. Sometimes all we can do in response is to take a deep breath and to take a next step, even when we are not quite sure where that step is going to lead us. Then Jesus speaks about the intimacy of God with us every step of the way, by using another very fond image. He says, "He knows every hair on your head and he has numbered them all." To know that God has such a close connection with each of us somehow enables us to endure. If you notice, that word "endurance" is hidden away in the body of this Gospel story. Faith is endurance. And sometimes life itself can only be endured. There is very little about it we can be thankful for, very little about it that puts us at ease, very little about it that gives us hope. The same God who has his eye on every sparrow has his eye on each of us. That knowledge can enable us to endure.

Yet realistic is our Lord. Life is difficult, and the Christian life can be even more difficult. But because of God's presence with us in the darkness and the light, in the pain and the joy, in the peace and the chaos, somehow, as God's children, as Christ's followers, we are empowered to stand up in the face of life and be witnesses to the one irreducible fact, that God is with us in the midst of it all. This awareness does not change the circumstances of life and it does not prevent difficulties, yet somehow this assurance gives us the power to endure and carry on. Thanks be to God for that mysterious gift!

Life Is Not Fair

MATTHEW 20:1–16

Jesus said, "For the kingdom of heaven is like a landowner who went out early in the morning to hire laborers for his vineyard. After agreeing with the laborers for the usual daily wage, he sent them into his vineyard. When he went out about nine o'clock, he saw others standing idle in the marketplace; and he said to them, 'You also go into the vineyard, and I will pay you whatever is right.' So they went. When he went out again about noon and about three o'clock, he did the same. And about five o'clock he went out and found others standing around; and he said to them, 'Why are you standing here idle all day?' They said to him, 'Because no one has hired us.' He said to them, 'You also go into the vineyard.' When evening came, the owner of the vineyard said to his manager, 'Call the laborers and give them their pay, beginning with the last and then going to the first.' When those hired about five o'clock came, each of them received the usual daily wage. Now when the first came, they thought they would receive more; but each of them received the usual daily wage. And when they received it, they grumbled against the landowner, saying, 'These last worked only one hour, and you have made them equal to us who have borne the burden of the day and the scorching heat.' But he replied to one of them, 'Friend, I'm doing you no wrong; did you not agree with me for the usual daily wage? Take what belongs to you and go; I choose to give to this last the same as I give to you. Am I not allowed to do what I choose with what belongs to me? Or are you envious because I am generous?' So the last will be first, and the first will be last."

*I*t isn't fair at all, is it? In fact, it's an outrage, this parable which our Lord holds up before us for our reflection this week. It's not fair at all. The more I have been reflecting on this story in my own life, the more I have become aware that life itself is not fair much of the time. So this parable has a connection with our life and is not just a strange story which is hard to understand.

Jesus had a marvelous way of reorienting our thinking and bringing us face to face with truths which God would have us know. This story is an intriguing example of Jesus' ability to open us to levels of meaning that we would not be able to discern on our own. It is a perplexing incident which only Matthew recounts, and he probably remembered it because he was an accountant. He was fascinated by Jesus' talking about business or financial matters. But when he relates the incident to us, we find that it just doesn't make any sense. We ask, "Do you mean I should run my business this way?" Of course not. This parable is not about labor relations, or minimum wage, or Economics 101. Its purpose is to unveil to us a truth which is above our normal way of thinking about life.

The main point Jesus is making here focuses on the astounding generosity of God. It blows our minds; it defies our imaginations… God's astounding generosity. And no, it doesn't make any sense to us, but its message is profound. The story tells us something about ourselves as well. In this highly competitive society in which we live, we find that people either compare us to other folks, or we measure our value by comparing ourselves to other people. It is very easy for us to be envious of those people who seem to have more than we have for some reason, people who have it easier than we do, and people who do not seem to suffer the same kinds of things we suffer. When we look at life in this way, we find that envy and jealousy can quickly infect our hearts. So Jesus is warning us in this story about the spiritual poisons which can issue from our being envious, resentful, or jealous. Yet we are, aren't we?

Jesus' purpose is to help us avoid the twin pitfalls of the life of faith. Those pitfalls are either spiritual arrogance (a sense that we are better than others), or spiritual inferiority (a sense that we are less than others). Jesus declares that in God's gracious economy we are equal recipients of God's love, which is lavishly poured out on us all the time. There is nothing we can do to earn that love. We have no merit to bring before God. God never gives any of us what we deserve, only vastly more.

When we come face to face with this truth and see our own lives as basking in God's grace, which is a limitless resource, then Jesus asks us to live our lives on a different plane. Instead of comparison, competition, jealously, and envy our Lord tells us there is only one antidote to those spiritual illnesses and that antidote is gratitude. We are to live our lives not by comparing them to others, but by taking seriously the grace and gifts which God lavishes upon us day in and day out. This is the secret to spiritual health which our Lord holds up before us. So the one question which hangs at the end of this amazing story is: How grateful are you for the life God has given you to live?

Praying for Rain

LUKE 11:1–13

Jesus was praying in a certain place, and after he had finished, one of his disciples said to him, "Lord, teach us to pray, as John taught his disciples." And Jesus said to them, "When you pray say: Father, hallowed be your name. Your kingdom come. Give us each day our daily bread. And forgive us our sins, for we ourselves forgive everyone indebted to us. And do not bring us to the time of trial." And he said to them, "Suppose one of you has a friend, and you go to him at midnight and say to him, 'Friend, lend me three loaves of bread; for a friend of mine has arrived, and I have nothing to set before him.' And he answers from within, 'Do not bother me; the door has already been locked, and my children are with me in bed; I cannot get up and give you anything.' I tell you even though he will not get up and give him anything because he is his friend, at least because of his persistence he will get up and give him whatever he needs. So I say to you, ask, and it will be given you; search, and you will find; knock, and the door will be opened for you. For everyone who asks receives, and everyone who searches finds, and for everyone who knocks, the door will be opened. Is there anyone among you who, if your child asks for a fish, will give a snake instead of a fish? Or if the child asks for an egg, will give a scorpion? If you then, who are evil, know how to give good gifts to your children, how

much more will the heavenly Father give the Holy Spirit
to those who ask him!"

*I*t had been a long, hot, and especially dry summer. The
drought was reaching its peak and the crops were just before
dying. A country preacher was going throughout the small
town saying that he was going to hold a service to pray for rain
the next day at one of the largest fields in the county and he
wanted everybody to be there to help him. The next morning he
got up early, went to the edge of the field, and watched a huge
crowd gather at the fence line. Attention was on the preacher as
he jumped up on a hay wagon and said, "Brothers and sisters,
we are here today to pray for rain." "Yea, amen, brother, that's
why we are here," said the crowd. The preacher looked around
and said, "Is your faith sufficient for this task?" "Amen, brother,
amen, that's why we are here; yes it is." He looked around some
more and said, "I still have one more question to ask of you."
They looked at one another a bit puzzled and perplexed as he
asked, "Brothers and sisters, where are your umbrellas?"

The disciples had watched Jesus go away many times to
pray. In the two years they had walked the dusty roads with him
they had been perplexed at times when he would wander off by
himself. He would even disappear from great crowds of people
and go off to pray. When he would come back his closest friends
would always notice there was a new sense of resolve about him.
There was a new calm, a new clarity of purpose, a new serenity
in his face. Something powerful occurred in those experiences
of prayer even though no one was there to eavesdrop or write
down what Jesus said when he went away to pray. His closest

friends knew something very special had happened to him, and they longed for a similar experience in their own lives. So they said to him after he returned from this time of prayer, "Lord, we want what you have. Teach us also to pray."

Jesus knew that this was a true heart hunger which his closest friends felt. In his compassion, he knew that this was a heart hunger felt by everyone in the same intense way…a deep longing to have prayer be fulfilling, inspirational, strengthening, clarifying, and cheering. The disciples needed this experience, so they asked him for it. Jesus knew what they needed and he responded accordingly.

Several years ago *Newsweek* hired Gallup Poll to do a survey of American citizens. I don't know how many thousands of people were interviewed but over a course of months various kinds of people were questioned about the place and meaning of prayer in their lives. The reporter discovered that people utilized many varieties of prayer, from desperate cries for help when backs were against the wall, to the quiet Evensong as a way to nurture our souls. The survey revealed that eighty-eight percent of the American public prays regularly and frequently, not just in crisis. Answers ranged from the simple saying of a blessing at mealtime to lengthy daily devotional expressions.

The reporter discovered something startling after realizing that eighty-eight percent of people do pray. He found upon further questioning that only twenty-nine percent of those people who prayed had a frequent consistent experience of God within their prayer life. Many people's prayers either stopped at the ceiling or left them feeling empty and unanswered. He also discovered that twenty-one percent of the people who prayed never had any experience of God at all in their prayers…a one-way street, simply with no response.

Difficult it is to have a prayer life as Jesus had for himself, and yet deep in our heart of hearts and in the depths of our soul that is something we all long for. No matter how good life is, there is a mystical yearning for us to be closely connected with God in order for life to be full. Rabbi Harold Kushner wrote a book some years ago called *When All You Have Is Not Enough*. In this book the Jewish rabbi reminded the American public that, in the midst of all the "affluenza" we experience in our culture, there is a consequent spiritual emptiness that is apparent. The remedy for this spiritual disease is a close connection with God.

Jesus knew this about his friends then and he knows this to be true about us today. So when he heard his disciples' request, "Lord, teach us to pray," he knew they were not asking for a series of phrases to be memorized; they were asking for a relationship to be realized. Consequently, he did not give them a long formal prayer. Instead he gave them a very simple petition which is now known traditionally as the Lord's Prayer, the Our Father, as the Roman Catholic Church calls this prayer.

If you notice in this morning's reading, the rendition we heard is much shorter than the one we will use later in our liturgy. It is also much shorter than the one Matthew gives us. Even though Luke writes later than Matthew, most biblical scholars think that Luke really gives us the original form of Jesus' response to this request, "Lord, teach us to pray."

Notice how he begins: one word, which sets the stage for the whole prayer, "Father." This was a revolutionary word in religious circles. Never before had God been addressed as Father. When Jesus used the Hebrew word, "Abba," for "Father," he was using a word which connotes all of the best of human fatherhood. Really what he was saying was to call God "Daddy." Have you ever dared to begin your prayer life, "Daddy"? This is exactly what Jesus recommends we do in order to get the sense of intimacy, connection, and closeness with God which our souls crave. Father...Jesus wanted us to imagine any time we said our prayers that we would climb up into the lap of the most trusting, lovable, compassionate, embracing parent and say, "Daddy, here's who I am and here's what I need." This truly is a revolutionary way of beginning to understand the life of prayer.

Then do you notice what Jesus said in those terse phrases that follow? The first thing is to focus our minds and our hearts on God, not on what we need. Most of the time our prayers begin with what we need, don't they? But Jesus very wisely says that in order for prayer to be spiritually fulfilling it must begin with a recognition of God's goodness, God's generosity, God's loving kindness, God's mercy, God's holiness; then we will be in the proper frame of mind to ask for whatever we need, and to express how we feel. So first of all we set our minds, hearts, and spirits on God's presence in our life as our intimate father. Next we begin to ask for the three essentials of spiritual health.

We need to be very careful here in understanding prayer. Jesus did not see prayer as a blank check sent to each of us on which we could write anything our hearts desired. We know life doesn't revolve around our needs. But Jesus says there are three things which when faithfully requested will be granted to us. The first thing is daily bread. The Greek is very explicit here.

If we translated this correctly it would read, "Give us each day our daily bread for this day." Nothing could be more emphatic than those words, referring to present needs only, not securing ourselves for the future, not stocking up our cupboard for next week, and not fattening our bank accounts for the lean years. Give us this day bread that we need to sustain us for this period of time. This insight might help us temper and discipline what we ask of God so glibly. Give us this day our daily bread.

As food is essential for our bodies, forgiveness is necessary for our souls. So forgiveness is the second petition we are to make because we all need it as much as we need daily bread. When we hurt others or when we are hurt by others, forgiveness is the only resource that will sustain us. We can become so embittered, so isolated, so negative, if we are not able to forgive. Jesus knows the necessity of this marvelous gift of forgiveness. But there are times when our own hurts and wounds are too deep for us to muster the strength or energy to forgive. So Jesus says, "Pray for forgiveness, because your Father who delights in giving you good things will give you far more than you ever imagined was there." We must pray for forgiveness because it is as necessary for our spiritual health as breathing in and breathing out are necessary for our physical health.

Thirdly, we are to pray for endurance. Notice how this prayer evolves. It is really a mystery to me. Jesus' wisdom is so powerful here. First of all he talks about present needs; then he talks about past hurts; and now he is talking about future adversities. Jesus is not saying here that prayer is going to protect us from all the bad things that are going to happen to us in this life. He does not guarantee us such protection. If we base our prayer life on the fact that we will be protected from all pain, our faith is going to be crushed by that perspective. Jesus is teaching us to ask God for the spiritual strength to endure when the circumstances of life seem to turn against us.

The longer I live and the more I experience, the more I equate faith with endurance. I mean simply being able to endure pain, disappointment and setback, the death of dreams, the death of people, those things that are going to happen to all of us. Jesus knew that they were going to happen to all of us. He is encouraging us to pray for strength to endure so the adversity will not be great enough to crush our spirit and dash our hopes. God will give us what we need. "Expect that," he says.

Then he asks those of us who are parents, as he says something like this: "You folks who have children, if your child comes to you and says, 'I need something to eat, give me some fish.' Do you reach inside a drawer and pull out a poisonous snake and put it in the hands of your child? Or when your child says, 'I would like a scrambled egg,' do you put on the plate of that child a poisonous scorpion? No, you do not. Think about this then, imperfect and sinful as you are, how much good you are willing to do for children. God is going to do manifold times more than you do in an overwhelmingly generous way."

We are to ask and we will be heard; we are to seek and we are going to be found; and we are to knock and God is going to open his spirit to us. Then we are going to be supplied our daily needs. We are going to be given the power to forgive and be forgiven, and we are going to be given the strength to endure the adversities of life. This is what prayer meant to Jesus, and this is why his life was so energized every time he prayed. He knew what prayer could mean and he knew what his people needed. And so from now on when you pray your prayers or when you pray the Lord's Prayer, I hope you will remember to bring your umbrellas. Amen.

Just Who Do You Think You Are?

HEBREWS 2:1–8

That is why we are bound to pay all the more heed to what we have been told, for fear of drifting from our course. For if God's word spoken through the angels had such force that any violation of it, or any disobedience, met with its proper penalty, what escape can there be for us if we ignore so great a deliverance? This deliverance was first announced through the Lord, and those who heard him confirmed it to us, God himself adding his testimony by signs and wonders, by miracles of many kinds, and by gifts of the Holy Spirit distributed at his own will. For it is not to angels that he has subjected the world to come, which is our theme. There is somewhere this solemn assurance: What is man, that you should remember him, a man, that you should care for him? You made him for a short while subordinate to the angels; with glory and honor you crowned him; you put everything in subjection beneath his feet.

Just who do you think you are? Many of us wonder and worry about that question a lot. Some of us turn it entirely over to others to tell us who we are and how we are to live. We might turn that question in on ourselves and come to a conclusion, which leads us to think too highly of ourselves. At the same time I'm afraid some of us think too lowly of ourselves. Listen to what Holy Scripture tells us about ourselves. The truth is hidden in the eighth Psalm. The Old Testament truth about us is, "When I consider your heavens, the work of your fingers, the moon and the stars that you have set in their courses, what are human beings that you should be mindful of them and that you should seek them out? You have made them but little lower than the angels. You adorn them with glory and honor. You give them mastery over the works of your hands. You put all things under their feet." And now from the New Testament, hidden away in the reading from the Letter to the Hebrews, "What are human beings that you are mindful of them or mortals that you care for them? You have made them for a little while lower than the angels. You have crowned them with glory and honor, subjecting all things under their feet." Now in subjecting all things to them, God left nothing outside their control. That's us. This is what Holy Scripture tells us about ourselves and that is right heady stuff, isn't it? But it's also dangerous at the same time.

God took a great risk when God put everything in our control and this is exactly what happened when we received this gift of life. All the time there ever will be for us is ours to control. All of our energy, all of our talents, all of our money, all of our interests, all of those aspects of our humanity are ours to control. Herein lies the danger, because in giving us this freedom to choose, God has given each of us the important responsibility to make a decision about how we will use the life which is ours to manage. All of us struggle with this decision, because it is good and wonderful to know that everything is mine and I can do with it whatever I wish. But there is a dark voice in each of our souls that tells us we should use our power to do only what is good for us. Instead of being willing to give away what is given, the voice tells us to keep it, to hoard it. God has given us this awful freedom to choose between these voices.

A very profound contemporary theologian, Simone Weil, reminds us that God chose not to become everything in order that each of us may become something. We are called to be co-creators with God and not simply consumers of his creation.

There are several other truths hidden away in these scriptural reflections. The first truth declares that no one deserves all we have been given. No one has earned it. Everything we have and all that we are, are pure gifts to us. We had no choice in that. Our Creator who made us and then gave us control over all creation gives us this gift of life. The image of God was created in each of us, along with all of the other aspects of our humanity which make us who we are. The image of God has to do with the nature of God. What is the nature of God to you? The nature of God to me is *giver* and this is the one characteristic that is revealed about God from the beginning of the Old Covenant to the end of the New.

Wherever God is spoken of, it is the God who gave. The nature of God is giver, and if we are serious about living into the image which God has placed in each of us, then it seems to me that our lives are to be more focused on giving than controlling and hoarding. Jesus Christ spoke directly to this truth when he said that if we are serious about finding our lives then we are going to have to be free to give them away. This is the way of blessedness and this is the way to spiritual health. Blessedness is the result of our living as created in the image of God.

I'm reading a wonderful book right now called *My Grandfather's Blessings: The Story of Strength, Refuge, and Belonging.* If you want to read something that will pick you up and send you on your way, this book will do it. Rachel Ramen, a physician whose sole mission in life is to care for people who are dying of cancer, is its author. Her purpose is not to cure them or treat them, but to give as much meaning to their dying as she can. Even though she is medically trained, this is her unique ministry in life. She speaks eloquently through these pages about the fact that each of us has the power to bless life. Do you ever think about yourself in that way, that God gives you the power to bless life? Wow, that's astounding! But just as we have the power to bless life we have the power to curse it. The way to bless life is to be free to lose control of it and to give ourselves away. The way to curse life and all of those around us is to hoard ourselves and control ourselves and refuse to give ourselves away.

Each of us in this place is given the freedom to grow into the nature and image of God, and we are going to be hearing a question put before us for the next two months, maybe ad nauseum, some of you would say. The question is, will you grow? Simply put. Are we willing to grow into the nature of God created in us? If we are willing to grow into this nature we are going to be called to give away more and more of ourselves. There are no boundaries to this giving.

All of the time in the world God gives to us, all of this energy, all of these gifts, all of this money, all of this experience. God has placed a wealth in each of our lives and we are going to be facing squarely this question: *Where am I at this point in my growth, and am I willing to grow beyond where I am at this moment?* This is an unsettling question, but a question that can be a catalyst to lead us into a deeper spiritual health.

We have, my friends, the power to choose. Everything is in our control. What choice will we make? Will we bless or will we curse? Are we willing to grow? So now, just who do you think you are?

Living through the Worst of Times

JOHN 6:53–59

Jesus said to them, "Very truly, I tell you, unless you eat the flesh of the Son of Man and drink his blood, you have no life in you. Those who eat my flesh and drink my blood have eternal life, and I will raise them up on the last day; for my flesh is true food and my blood is true drink. Those who eat my flesh and drink my blood abide in me, and I in them. Just as the living Father sent me, and I live because of the Father, so whoever eats me will live because of me. This is the bread that came down from heaven, not like that which your ancestors ate, and they died. But the one who eats this bread will live forever." He said these things while he was teaching in the synagogue at Capernaum.

Let us pray: Gracious Father, we pray for your Holy Catholic Church. Fill it with all truth and in all truth with all peace. Where it is corrupt, purify it; where it is in error, direct it; where in anything it is amiss, reform it; where it is right, strengthen it; where it is in want, provide for it; where it is divided, reunite it. For the sake of Jesus Christ, thy Son, our Savior. AMEN

For my flesh is true food and my blood is true drink, and whoever receives my body and my blood receives a new quality of life. You have no idea how much comfort these words have given me this past week as I have reflected on them for myself and have struggled to reflect them to you in a way that I hope will give you some comfort and some strength. These last two weeks, since the General Convention of our church decided to ordain Gene Robinson as bishop of New Hampshire, have been the worst weeks of forty years of ministry for me. I am weary, I am worried, I am angry, I am frustrated, I am bewildered, and I think at the bottom of it all I am grief-stricken. I have listened to your anguish and I have absorbed your pain and I will continue to do that. But I *am* weary and perplexed, disappointed and hurt.

At the bottom of my sadness is my awareness that the light has gone out in this parish momentarily. We have become preoccupied. We have been consumed. We have been a beacon of hope for this community in the past and we have offered ourselves in ways that only God could have directed. But we are shattered at this moment and we have nothing to offer to anybody else. This is at the heart of my sadness. I am also aware that this conflict we face has divided husbands and wives and has caused fear for parents on behalf of their children. And so, I have drawn great hope from these words of our Lord.

I know when we are shocked and shattered as we are, it is a very normal human response to want to take some direct action. And we are in danger of behaving in ways which may not be God's will if pain and anger motivate our action, both as individuals and as a parish family. These words from St. John's Gospel give me some comfort in that they are not spoken in a cozy living room setting. Jesus does not write them as he sits serenely by a lake and reflects on life. These words are born out of turmoil.

Capernaum was a city in awful conflict. People were already beginning to find ways they could kill Jesus because of what he was saying and what he was doing. So when he gives us these words of hope, he too is writing, speaking, and living in the midst of great pain. I can only imagine what our Lord's heart must be doing at this moment because of what is happening to his people. I know what my heart is doing and if I multiply that a thousand times maybe that can get close to what is going on in our Lord's heart. I do not know for sure. But I am lonely and I am perplexed because I do not know what is the right thing to do at this moment. And as we face this crisis in the weeks and months to come—I know we will be in crisis that long—I find in these words from our Lord today a strength which will keep me going, keep me from sinking in the mire of our controversy.

These words taken from St. John's Gospel are written for a purpose. John has a wonderful way of lifting our spirits, lifting our thoughts beyond the human. This is his purpose in writing that unique Gospel and at this moment in time it is my favorite of the four. As I go through life I find that one week Luke is my favorite and the next week Mark and the next week Matthew. Right now, John's is my favorite Gospel because John helps my spirit soar; John helps me to lift my head above the groundswell of feelings which swirl around me hour by hour. Not only have I been open to your pain over these last two weeks, but I have buried two good friends, baptized five babies, and helped two couples get married. This shift of feeling in the midst of the rollercoaster called life tears me to pieces normally, but all of that has happened against the backdrop of this pain we share right now. Therefore, I have found comfort and solace in St.

John's perspective which I have never found before. I offer it to you as a vantage point.

Nobody knows for sure how this crisis will be resolved, and I would distrust anybody who says he or she does. As we go into the future I do not have any faith in you; I do not have any faith in me. I know everything St. Paul has said. For forty-five years I have studied his mind and his behavior and I have great respect for his commitment and his attempts to create theology. But my life is not committed to St. Paul; my life is committed to Jesus Christ and it is his mind, it is his heart, it is his behavior that will guide me in my daily living. I do wonder in this instance what is going on in the heart and the mind of our Lord Christ.

Back in the nineties we had that trite little expression, the acronym WWJD, on our bumper stickers (and you know how I detest bumper-sticker theology). But it was there and we wore bracelets, WWJD. What Would Jesus Do? My beloved friends, I would suggest at this point that these four words give us the vantage point we should be living in. What would Jesus do in the midst of this crisis as his people are divided against one another, as people are being vilified and misunderstood? What would Jesus do in our midst if he stood right here this morning and heard from us our own responses to the crisis we face? I know we want to do something. But right now when we are caught up in the midst of the intensity of this situation, it is not the time to do something. It is time for us to be still, to let St. John's perspective on our Lord Christ help our hearts and minds to soar to a new level.

When traditionalists and artists have tried to symbolize St. John and the impact that he had on life, do you know what they chose? They chose an eagle. Because an eagle's majesty and beauty are typified in its soaring above life. I think we are offered a gift this morning…to have our minds, our spirits, and our hearts soar a bit so that we can get a better perspective and regain our bearings. This parish is not going to survive on anything that you or I as individuals think we should do; and I think we need to come face to face with this reality and be humbled by it. And I think we are being called upon now to be more open to God's Holy Spirit than we ever have been. When Jesus was facing the end of his life, he said, "I cannot tell you all the things you need to know now; your minds could not handle it. But God is going to send a Spirit who is going to teach you all things and I want you to be open to that Spirit." That was our Lord's last wish for his church. So today and tomorrow and next month and maybe next year, I hope you will allow your heart and your mind to be in a different place. When you think about the issues that confront us, I beg you to think about them with the mind of Christ. And when you deal with your own fears, I beg you to love with the heart of Christ. And when you get so preoccupied with your own perspective and your own feelings, I beg you to serve as the hands of Christ in this world. This humility will be the source of our healing; this openness will be the source of our strength. This sense of servanthood will keep us connected with one another in this part of Christ's Holy Catholic Church.

Loved into Being

JOSHUA 24:1–2, 14–15

Joshua assembled all the tribes of Israel at Shechem. He summoned the elders of Israel, the heads of families, the judges and officers. When they presented themselves before God, Joshua said to all the people, "Now hold the Lord in awe, and serve Him in loyalty and truth. Put away the gods your fathers served beyond the Euphrates. This is Joshua speaking to all the people. But if it does not please you to serve the Lord, choose here and now whom you will serve. But I and my family, we shall serve the Lord...."

JOHN 6:51, 60–69

Jesus said, "I am the living bread that came down from heaven. Whoever eats of this bread will live forever." When many of his disciples heard it, they said, "This teaching is difficult; who can accept it?" But Jesus, being aware that his disciples were complaining about it, said to them, "Does this offend you? Then what if you were to see the Son of Man ascending to where he was before? It is the spirit that gives life; the flesh is useless. The words that I have spoken to you are spirit and life. But among you there are some who do not believe." For Jesus knew from the first who were the ones who did not believe, and who was the one that would betray him. And he said, "For this reason I have told you that no one can come to me unless it is granted by the Father." Because of this many of his disciples turned back and no longer went about with him. So Jesus asked the twelve, "Do you also wish to go away?" Simon Peter answered him, "Lord, to whom can we go? You have the words of eternal life. We have come to believe and know that you are the Holy One of God."

Today we celebrate! We celebrate the beginning of this parish one hundred and fifty-five years ago when God gathered a tiny band of eleven Episcopalians somewhere on this city block and established the congregation called Advent. Also this day we celebrate a powerful present, which shall unfold into a glorious future as we assess this congregation's strengths. Look around at all the precious children here! Be aware of the gifts and talents represented here. We do celebrate a most powerful present life together, my friends. But we also anticipate a future full of hope, because we stand in awe before the mystery of unimagined ministries into which God has yet to call us.

Today we celebrate. And in a moment we are going across the street to dedicate to God a monument. This monument demonstrates God's goodness to us in our past, our present, and our future. But we are also going to celebrate your generosity, because that caused our magnificent structure to come into being. We also offer a gift of ourselves this day to the generations which will follow us in this place and make up the future congregation called Advent.

What a marvelous backdrop these readings are today for this celebration! Gifts in themselves, the readings from Joshua out of the Old Testament, and the words of our Lord himself recorded by St. John. There is a theme which runs between these two readings which is a perfect one for us on this momentous day…a theme highlighting devotion, commitment, loyalty, faithfulness, and servanthood…a theme I pray will carry us forward from this day through all the years to come.

Joshua's words to us are most inspirational. Joshua is an old man; he has been leading the Israelites for most of his adult life. He has brought them to the point of settling into the Promised Land. Here he gives his farewell address to a great gathering of all the tribes, all the leaders, all the people who have followed him, all the children who will carry his banner into the future. He addresses that great gathering at Shechem, a holy place, a gathering of all the peoples of God, and he reminds them, as they settle in, they need to be very careful to remember that they depend upon God alone, not on their power, not on their skill, and not on their wisdom.

On that great day at Shechem, Joshua reminds his people of God's lavish goodness to them in times past. He reminds them that once they were not a community, but that God somehow drew them together under the leadership of Abraham and started them out on their long, arduous, sometimes despairing journey toward the Promised Land. He recalls that once when they were enslaved in Egypt, God liberated them from an oppressive power, which had enslaved them and kept them from being the people God called them to be. Furthermore, he tells them that upon freedom from slavery, God had led them into the wilderness but had not abandoned them. There God gave them the gift of the commandments by which they would begin to shape their lives and their values. He says it was God who promised the land and gave it to them, and defended them along the way against some vicious enemies. And God brought them to the Promised Land and gave them the responsibility to take care of it.

Finally, he reminds those people to look back and remember that they are who they are because God called them and loved them into being. Then he presents a dilemma. He warns them to be careful, saying that there will be many gods beckoning for their allegiance. These foreign gods will be asking them to place their trust in them, so they will have to be careful about whom they will serve. Joshua stands up boldly and declares, "But as for me, I and my house, we will continue to serve the Lord God, and you this day must choose whom you will serve."

Joshua issues a challenging question for us as we stand together at this time of celebration. Whom will we serve as we go into the future? Here Jesus' words connect with what Joshua was saying. As Joshua had reminded the people of times past and God's presence in the present, Jesus also said, "I have come to fulfill all that God had in store for you. I have come to give you a higher standard of living than you could ever imagine. This new quality of life is based on my life, which will be with you forever. And as you go into your future it is going to be more and more necessary for you to take me into the very core of your being."

This Gospel for today is sad in many ways. Jesus was beginning to declare the demands of the Christian way of living. He was beginning to talk about love as the greatest of all virtues. As he spoke about servanthood and sacrifice, many listeners became uneasy with that part of the Gospel. He was great for them when he could feed them all the bread and fish they could eat. But many started to turn away when he talked about the necessity of living the life of love.

Jesus did admit that this new standard of living would be very difficult to fulfill. His presence dwelling in us gives us the ability to do his will. So he talked about feeding us, literally feeding us his body and his blood. And in so doing Jesus was saying that he wanted to claim us at the very core of our being, as individuals and as a parish. If we acknowledge his claim upon our lives and are loyal to his way of life, it is going to be necessary for us to feed regularly on what he has to give us. In effect Jesus was saying, "I want you to drink in my truth and to live by it. I want you to absorb my love and let it motivate your every action. I want you to open yourself up and set aside all your agendas and your preconceived notions about the Christian way of life. I want you to take into yourself my power, a power which you will then use for good and healing and hope in this world." And many backed away and followed him no more.

But, my friends, we are here today to recommit ourselves to the following of our Lord. If that magnificent structure across the street is to have any value at all, it will have value only as it enables us to live according to Christ's truth, to incarnate his love in this world, and to give his power away for the hope and the healing of this community. Bread is only bread when it is broken and given away. Wine is only wine when it is poured out and shared. That's a hard saying, but it is the way our Lord calls us to live. Echoing through the sands of time, Joshua says, "Choose this day whom you will serve." And Jesus says, "Will you also go away?" My prayer for each of us is that we will say as Simon Peter said, "Lord, where in the world are we going to go? You have the words of eternal life, and it is to you that we devote ourselves anew, for you are the center of all that is." Amen.

A Ladder and a Lantern

MATTHEW 22:34–46

When the Pharisees heard that Jesus had silenced the Sadducees they gathered together, and one of them, a lawyer, asked him a question to test him. "Teacher, which commandment in the law is the greatest?" And Jesus said to him, "You shall love the Lord your God with all your heart, with all your soul, and with all your mind." This is the greatest and first commandment. The second is like it: "You shall love your neighbor like yourself. On these two commandments hang all the law and the prophets." Now while the Pharisees were gathered together, Jesus asked them these questions: "What do you think of the Messiah? Whose son is he?" They said to him, "The son of David." He said to them, "How is it then that David by the Spirit calls him Lord, saying, 'The Lord said to my Lord, sit at my right hand, until I put your enemies under your feet'? If David thus calls him Lord, how can he be his son?" No one was able to give him the answer, nor from that day did anyone dare to ask him any more questions.

Today is Commitment Sunday in our life together…a time when we make real and concrete our devotion to God… Commitment Sunday. What does the word "commitment" mean to you? It has many levels of meaning, doesn't it? And if we go to the wordsmiths who help us define language in our culture, we find there are many definitions of this word, but most agree that commitment refers to the entrusting of oneself literally and figuratively to the charge of another...entrusting one's self literally and figuratively to the charge of another. Other experts define commitment as an act of giving beyond one's self to something or someone other than self, an act of entrusting, an act of giving. This is what commitment means. But if we look at this word through the lens of Holy Scripture, we find that commitment really is nothing more than a four-letter word: love. This definition is from the lips of our Lord and from the wisdom of his life. Commitment is equated with love. In order to understand this fully we need to get some sense of what is going on in this Gospel incident for today.

This is one of the last conversations that Jesus has with anybody, this confrontation he has there with the Pharisees. He has been engaged in much heated debate recently, and this encounter seems to be the culmination of that controversy. So a spokesperson of the Pharisees (referred to as a lawyer) approaches Jesus. Here we need a clear understanding of this word "lawyer."

We usually think about civil law, litigation, courtrooms, judges, and trials when we think of lawyers. This is not what is implied here, however. When the word "lawyer" is used in scripture, it refers to one who is an expert in religious matters, one who knows everything about the religious regulations of the holy life. So this person who steps up is an expert in Jewish law, but he seems confused about what he knows. He knows that Jewish law has 613 commands; 248 of those are positive commands, which correspond to parts of the human body. Exactly 365 of those commands are negative and are determined by the number of days of the year. So, there are 248 parts to the whole body, added to the 365 days in a year, giving a total of 613 commands to live the holy religious life.

Now we can understand how this fellow was perplexed, can't we? He knows all the rules, yet he knows he cannot begin to fulfill all of them. He wants something a little simpler, a little more direct. So he goes up to Jesus, because he admires his wisdom, and he knows he is a good teacher, and he asks for a little clarification, a little simplification. "Sir," he said, "is there any way we can distill these 613 regulations into a more workable, livable list?" Jesus said, "Yes, there is a summary of all of these," and Jesus draws this summary out of the Old Testament, as he reiterates the commandment to love.

There is a sense of wholeness about this act of loving which is declared in this Gospel. I am sorry our translation today is so passive. The real rendering of the Greek has much more muscle and much more power than "you shall." That is too permissive, almost as if Jesus has given a good suggestion and said, "Why don't you think about this for awhile and if it is comfortable, you can start doing it." This is a commandment that Jesus gives in this summary, not something for us to think about and consider, but something for us to live up to. He states clearly that all of Jewish law is contained in the law of loving.

Loving is that act of entrusting; it is that act of giving beyond oneself. Think about this for just a minute. We are in the context of Eucharist. Have you ever thought about the fact that when you come up here to this altar rail, and you open up your hands, that God entrusts himself into your hands? That is exactly what is happening here. God is entrusting himself into your charge, and when you leave this place God is entrusting the spread of his Gospel to each one of us who hears it and commits ourselves to it. Now that's high risk on God's part. But that is exactly what God does Sunday in and Sunday out; he entrusts his body and his blood to our care. And what a risk he takes! We must prove ourselves trustworthy as we assume this responsibility to love and to give, because this is who God is: the one who entrusts and the one who gives.

It is very important that we understand here what love really means. It can be even more confusing than commitment. First of all, love has nothing to do with feeling; it has everything to do with action. Love is not a misty-eyed sentimentality; love has to do with our behavior, with our action, with entrusting our whole being to God, and with our constant willingness to give ourselves away...whether we feel like it or not. Does love need to be commanded? You bet it does! There is not one of us in this place today who loves either naturally or easily. So the commandment to love is absolutely necessary in order for love to have any power in this world. Our love is measured by the act of our giving, whether we feel like it or not.

As I was struggling with this sermon over the past several weeks, I began to think back on my early learning. Where did I first learn the patterns of giving, which have guided my life for better than sixty years now? I began to remember that every week, starting from the time that I was five or six years old, my father would give me ten dimes as my weekly allowance. I understood when Daddy gave me those ten dimes, I was to put one dime in the children's offering envelope, which I was to take to church on Sunday morning and place in the alms basin.

Through this simple practice, my daddy was beginning to teach me how to live a loving and giving life.

I can tell you there were many Sundays I didn't want to put that dime in that little envelope and put it in the alms basin, because I had just found the right toy that I needed and it cost more than ninety cents. And yet, week in and week out, one of those ten dimes went into the offering plate. And I began to realize early in my life what commitment meant, what entrusting myself to another was all about, and that loving was as an act of giving beyond myself. My friends, our love is measured by how much we are willing to give. When you fill out your commitment card, it is going to be a clear indication of the depth of your love for our Lord, a concrete expression of your devotion to his mission in the world. We are being asked to give more and more and it will never be any different. When we take seriously this commandment to love, to entrust, to give beyond ourselves, we are doing so with the fervent hope that the mission of this congregation is going to be expanded and enlarged way beyond what it is at this moment.

Our mission cannot expand and enlarge unless we are willing to empower that with our own giving of ourselves; and that's risky business. Over the past eight or ten years you know how God has called us into missions which were scary for us; we did not know where we were going when we began; we did not know whether we could endure once we started; and we did not know what kind of good was going to come from all of the effort that we were pouring out. But we were willing to take a risk and we found that God empowered us to do what he called us to do.

So today as we stand in the midst of Commitment Sunday

we are reminded that where God blesses us, God also has great expectations of us. This is the commandment to love, and our love is measured by our giving. So when I think about what more God is going to ask of this parish, on the one hand it thrills me to think about that, and on the other it terrifies me. Because I don't know what the limit will be; I don't know what the extent of the risk is going to be, but I have a hunch that it is going to be an opportunity which will create some discomfort in our midst. And yet we are a people who are called to continue to entrust and to give beyond ourselves.

There is a story about an elderly priest who decided to retire. It was announced in the parish publication that his last sermon would be at a Vespers service. So the day came for his final service and the faithful worshipers were huddled up in the darkness of the cathedral waiting for the touching moment to occur.

They were very surprised when the old priest stepped through the back door of the cathedral and began to walk down the center aisle, carrying in one hand a ladder and in the other a lantern. He walked silently through the entire nave, through the chancel, and up into the sanctuary. He quietly put his ladder down at the foot of a life-sized crucifix which was hanging from the wall.

He climbed the ladder and held the lantern first to the right hand of the Crucified One that was shattered by the spike that was driven through it. He held it there for a moment and then moved it to the forehead of the Crucified One, which was gouged by the thorns on the crown. Then he moved the lantern to the left hand of the figure, to focus on the other shattered hand of the Christ. Slowly he moved the lantern down to the waist to the gaping hole in the figure's side, a hole made by a spear's point. Then he moved the lantern to the feet, which were also shattered by a spike driven into them.

The priest quietly climbed down from the ladder, walked back to the chancel steps, held up the lantern in the face of the congregation, and said, "Can we do any less?" and quietly left the church.

Can we do any less? On this Commitment Sunday, the question is for each of us. Can we do any less?

Good-bye and Hello
June 6, 2004

JOHN 16:5–13

"But now I am going to him who sent me; yet none of you asks me, 'Where are you going?' But because I have said these things to you, sorrow has filled your hearts. Nevertheless I tell you the truth: it is to your advantage that I go away, for if I do not go away, the Advocate will not come to you; but if I go, I will send him to you. And when he comes, he will prove the world wrong about sin and righteousness and judgment: about sin, because they do not believe in me; about righteousness, because I am going to the Father and you will see me no longer; about judgment, because the ruler of this world has been condemned.

"I still have many things to say to you, but you cannot bear them now. When the Spirit of truth comes, he will guide you into all the truth; for he will not speak on his own, but will speak whatever he hears, and he will declare to you the things that are to come."

*L*ife is about arrivals and departures, beginnings and endings, attachment and separation, closeness and distance, being near, being far away, saying hello and saying good-bye. This is what life is all about, and this truth about life is declared profoundly in the Gospel reading appointed for this day. This fact of life is also what this unique Sunday called Trinity Sunday proclaims for us and helps us celebrate. Yes, life is about arrivals and departures, beginnings and endings, closeness and distance, attachment and separation, saying hello and saying good-bye. I do not know if you have noticed it or not but these last four weeks the Gospel has been about this kind of reality. Jesus had been trying so hard to tell his closest friends that it was time; it was now time for him to go away. Sorrow filled their hearts when they thought about his leaving, and I can imagine that sorrow filled his heart as well as he faced his departure.

Trinity Sunday tells that life is a process, not a product. Life is always unfolding before us; there is always something new on the horizon. When Jesus talked to his friends about what was to come, he told them that were many truths that he could not teach them, truths they couldn't hear, understand, and actualize in their own lives. Jesus knew the whole truth was too much for them, so he told his followers near the end of his life that the experience with him was not all there is going to be.

Even the experience of the Crucifixion and the Resurrection is not all there is going to be. Even the Pentecostal experience which occurred after Easter is not all there is going to be. In fact, even the New Testament does not contain all there is going to be. "There is so much more truth out there yet to be unveiled," said Jesus, "and it is going to require more time and deeper experience for you to become more and more aware of all that God has in store for you." Jesus was speaking a very hopeful word here. He was telling his disciples that their life was just beginning; in spite of the sorrow of the ending, life itself was still going to unfold more fully in front of them.

Back to the Trinity…I will not waste your time or mine

trying to explain to you this ambiguous theological concept today because there is no way to do that. I would question anyone who dares to claim that they can explain fully the entirety of this mystery. There are some clues to its meaning, however. I have a little needlepoint plaque on the wall of my office which was given to me by a friend at the end of a long journey through tragedy which we took together. She came out at the end of her agony healed and a far richer, deeper person than she was before she encountered her loss. The needlepoint is a simple piece. It is a picture of a baby in a diaper sitting on the floor holding onto the string of a helium balloon, looking up at the balloon. The caption beneath that picture is: "Life is a mystery to be lived and not a problem to be solved."

This is the way it is with the Trinity. It is not a problem to be solved because we are never going to think it through and understand it fully. In fact it took the church almost four hundred years of terrible dispute to come to some flimsy idea about what the Trinity is, and that truth is still unfolding to this very moment. So the Trinity invites us into the mystery of life. It never expects us to understand it totally or explain it fully, because we will never be able to apprehend the whole truth that God has yet to reveal. But there is something very important about the Gospel for today and the doctrine of the Trinity which tell us something about life itself as it moves along. Jesus was saying that there is one coming after him who is going to open up to us a greater truth if we would only receive it. Jesus was telling his disciples that they would not be left comfortless, but would be given a powerful spirit to abide with them forever.

Here Jesus used the word "advocate," which is a legal word.

But if we are to understand its meaning fully, it is far more than a legal term. The word "advocate" really means "one who sticks close by you, a constant companion." This is precisely what God offers to us as we go through the beginnings and endings of our life with all of the joys and the pain of the journey. There is a spirit given to each of us which enables us not only to endure life's challenges and losses, but to live through them and come out on the other end with a deeper sense of the mystery of life than we had before. I say to people all the time that grief, if we let it do its work, will tenderize us. I believe that, because if we face our grief openly, the mystery of that experience makes us much more aware of and sensitive to the pain of others. This is a part of what Jesus was talking about in this Gospel, and also a part of what Trinity Sunday is holding up before each of us this day: God is to be found in the midst of all the change we are going to experience in our lives. God is going to be a close companion in the midst of it all, very close, closer than the air we breathe.

When I was a little boy something happened that revolutionized the motion picture industry. Somebody came up with the amazing invention of 3-D glasses. Does anybody remember 3-D glasses? I am glad to see those few nods out there! You don't know how comforting that is! The 3-D glasses, for those of us who have never heard of such, is now a primitive technology but was state of the art, cutting edge at the time. When you went to a certain movie you were given with the price of admission a little pair of cardboard glasses with two cellophane lenses in them, one green, one red. When the movie started and you put those glasses on, all of a sudden what used to be way out there, far away as the movie screen, appeared as close as the seat in front of you. It was a huge revolution! What a mystery that was to me as a child! This is exactly what the doctrine of the Trinity is trying to say to each of us today, that God is not remote and way off out there somewhere, but that God's loving, graceful, truthful spirit is right here, up close, to guide as we get confused in all of the meandering of life we are going to have to face.

Another translation of the word "advocate" is "communicator." God is one who will never withdraw communication from us, no matter how far we may wander away from his voice. But God is also educator, teacher in the midst of all the confusion that we are going to face in our lives. So what we say on this day, Trinity Sunday, is that God is not through with any of us yet; there is so much more to be unveiled. As we look at the life of faith we understand that we are only beginners. There is not one of us in this place who will ever receive a doctorate in discipleship, because we are always on the journey. We are always on the go; we are always in the process of learning more and more about what God calls us to be.

So as we celebrate what life is today, in all of its bittersweetness, we celebrate the fact that God will not let us go into this journey by ourselves, and that God will stand by to comfort and to guide and to give us a sense of his presence in spite of what life does to us. That, my friends, is reason to celebrate. This is the hope that we have as we go into our future. Thanks be to God. Amen.

Now and Forever
June 27, 2004

LUKE 9:51–62

When the days drew near for Jesus to be taken up, he set his face to go to Jerusalem. And he sent messengers ahead of him. On their way they entered a village of the Samaritans to make ready for him; but they did not receive him, because his face was set toward Jerusalem. When his disciples James and John saw it, they said, "Lord do you want us to command fire to come down from heaven and consume them?" But Jesus turned and rebuked them. Then they went on to another village. As they were going along the road, someone said to him, "I will follow you wherever you go." And Jesus said to him, "Foxes have holes, and birds of the air have nests; but the Son of Man has nowhere to lay his head." To another he said, "Follow me." But he said, "Lord, first let me go and bury my father." And Jesus said to him, "Let the dead bury their own dead; but as for you, go and proclaim the kingdom of God." Another said, "I will follow you, Lord, but let me first say farewell to those at my home." Jesus said to him, "No one who puts a hand to the plow and looks back is fit for the kingdom of God."

What does one say in one's last sermon? I have been haunted by this question for months now, and as I have tried to grapple with it my brain has been bombarded by lots of possibilities. The first thing that came to my mind was to use the pattern of David Letterman and come up with a list of those top ten things I always wanted to tell you that I never got around to. Well, I resisted that temptation. It took me too far afield from what I really wanted to have happen. So I started to think back to when we began this life a long time ago, to what I said in my first sermon to a tiny congregation in Rocky Mount, North Carolina. As I was wracking my brain, trying to remember what I said at that time, we had a surprise visit from four wonderful people who were parishioners in that small congregation in Rocky Mount. I said "Hot dog! Now they are going to be able to help me remember my first sermon." I asked them for their recollection, and they didn't remember a word I said the whole four years I was there. It didn't help a bit, but what a great humbling experience that was!

As I was cleaning the mess out of my office, I discovered a box of old sermons. I didn't know how old they were but believe it or not I used to write out sermons word by word. I used to underline certain words and I was very precise about my defining adjectives and my adverbs and careful not to split infinitives, so I thought, well, maybe there's a clue here. And as I read through some of those I threw them away pretty quickly. (I didn't spend a lot of time with them.) I discovered that they were written for another time and another place. I am not the same person and the context of life now is so different. But what I discovered digging through those musty old pages was that regardless of what I said then, the Gospel is still the same today. It was comforting for me to discover that through the years my own understanding of this Gospel has deepened and widened and I owe you a deep debt of gratitude for helping me grow through my life shared with you.

But the Gospel is the same, regardless of how much we might change and perceive it differently. Then I turned to this week's Gospel and I hoped to find there something upbeat that would carry us along. I didn't; this is a gloomy Gospel for today. And I wanted a message which would comfort us and move us through this time together, but try as I might, I couldn't avoid what this Gospel reading speaks loudly and clearly to each one of us. The Gospel that is read to you today expresses the same demanding, unrelenting, expectation as it always has done. The first people who heard it eons ago and those of us who hear it today find it to be the same challenge and demand it always has been. Our Lord never lets us off the hook in terms of how he expects us to live.

But let's get a sense of the Gospel. It tells us about a pivotal moment in Jesus' life. He is in one of those defining experiences in his own life. He is getting ready to leave what has been intimate, safe, familiar, and secure around the Sea of Galilee; where everyone knows his name; where everyone knows how to catch fish; everybody knows where to get the best fish in town; everybody knows who does what, and everything is safe and secure. Jesus is getting ready to leave Galilee to set his face toward a foreign land, a forbidding and frightful place. He is on the road and in the midst of a journey.

I think this can be comforting for each of us today. As we are on the road of life and as we are moving from one place to another in this time of great transition with its upheaval of feelings, I think we can find some guidance in what Jesus said to those people then that may help us in our journey now. Jesus was issuing some very strong challenges. I have a hunch that Jesus was going to the extreme in what he was saying, because if we took these challenges seriously we would have an empty house today. You wouldn't be here and I wouldn't be here because there is no one of us who could live up to the demands he continually makes upon us, setting our priorities aside and setting his priorities in the place of them. Unrealistic expectations Jesus had. If we took him literally and if we took the Gospel seriously, we would all be homeless paupers. Or we would all be street people who neglected their families. So we cannot take Jesus literally in terms of what he demands.

But there is a truth hidden away in those very strong challenges which will stretch us beyond where we are right now. Every time I reflect upon this Gospel, I think back to those coaches I played for and those teachers who taught me so much. The ones I remember most dramatically are the coaches and teachers who demanded of me far more than I was willing to give on my own. In demanding more from me than I thought I was capable of, they enabled me to accomplish more than I thought I was able. I think Jesus knows that truth. Here he sets before us challenges that on the one hand may daunt us and discourage us and get us to the point of saying, "Oh, it's no use, I'll give up." But Jesus trusts us to hear those challenges and to live more and more daily into them. This is the trust our Lord places in us. He pulls up the challenges to stretch us to grow beyond where we would grow on our own.

Jesus says something else that is so important to me. As he is on the road, he tells those people, "Don't you dare look back." The admonition here is for us not to let the past be an impediment to the future. Do not let memories stifle possibilities. Do not let the past, whether it's sorrowful or joyful, be an impediment to your future. And do not let your memories, painful or joyful, stifle the possibilities God has in store.

There's a word of hope hidden in the challenge. So be not dismayed, my friends, by the demands which are there. They have always been there, and there have always been groups of people who have picked them up and have gone on with them and have grown more than they thought they could ever grow as they faced the demands in front of them. I have said many times that you are people of miraculous expectations. Your Lord has magnificent expectations of you. The challenges are mighty, but you are a mighty people to respond. So rather than sink into depression today about this gloomy Gospel, let us hear what Martin Luther, that great Reformation theologian, said: "This life is not righteousness, but growth in righteousness; not health but healing; not being, but becoming; not rest, but exercise. We are not yet what we shall be, but we are growing toward it. The process is not yet finished, but it is going on. This is not the end, but it is the road. All does not yet gleam in glory, but everything is being purified." The Gospel now and forever. Amen.

Pieces of Clay

As we endeavor to fulfill God's will for us in this place, through the Cornerstone Campaign, I am going to ask you to join with me in thirty days of prayer. Thirty days of prayer focused on what kind of sacrifice God is requiring of you in order that we many respond to this new thing God is about to do in our midst. And I don't mean a tip or a token. I mean a sacrifice of all that we have been given, because when I think about the sacrifice of all those people who have gone before us here, when I think about all those people who sacrificed their lives in order that I might be at this point in my life, I am overwhelmed with gratitude. I am overwhelmed that so many were willing to give so much from which I have benefited. Aren't you?

———

St. Thérèse was an intriguing little Carmelite nun who lived in the French village of Lisieux. She never preached a sermon, and she never wrote a book, but she made a huge difference in both the monastic community and the village in which she lived. She knew as she began the Christian walk that she did not have many gifts and she was not going to have much influence. So she began to look for little ways in which she could cleanse the world, change or heal the world, and give the world more hope. Out of that intention she had a conversion experience in which all of a sudden she said, "I received God's love as infinite tenderness flooding me and the world."

Clearly her mission from that point forward was to use her life to share that infinite tenderness of God with everyone she met. That seems to be plausible for every one of us in this place today. To see our mission in this life as sharing the infinite tenderness of God with our spouse, with our children, our coworkers, our friends, with those who agree with us, those who disagree with us, and those who are our enemies, who hate us. The mission remains clear. We must find little ways to show the infinite tenderness of God to God's world.

—

Helen Keller is a heroine of mine, and when it comes to the topic of healing and wholeness, she has much to teach us. One day she went for a walk in the lovely woods with a friend of hers, and when she asked the friend what she had seen on the walk in the woods, the friend said "nothing in particular." Helen Keller said something like, "I wonder how it was possible to walk through the woods for an hour and see nothing in particular. I who cannot see at all find hundreds of things; the delicate symmetry of a leaf, the smooth skin of a silver birch, the shaggy bark of a pine. I who am blind can give one hint to those who see: use you eyes as if tomorrow you will be stricken blind. Hear the music of voices, the song of a bird, the mighty strains of an orchestra, as if tomorrow you will be deaf. Touch each object as if your sense of touch will be gone. Smell the perfume of flowers, taste with relish each morsel as if tomorrow you could never taste or smell again. Make the most of every sense every moment. Glory in all the facets and joys and beauties which the world continues to reveal to you." Helen Keller was whole, though not healed.

Afterword

The circular movement of the liturgical cycle repeats itself again and again, reminding us that our spiritual formation is constantly in flux. The Greek philosopher Epictetus once said that we never step into the same river twice. St. Paul told us that we are always in the process of working out our own salvation with fear and trembling. Life is always on the move, always facing us with beginnings and endings, opportunities and failures, fresh starts, and crushing losses. It is my hope that these sermons have carried us through some of the highs and the lows, the positives and the negatives which reality will offer us. In the midst of all the ebb and flow, the constancy of God's presence with us continues to shape and refine us, to enrich and develop us, to tenderize and strengthen us to be useful vessels carrying his love to everyone we touch. In the words of another great hymn, "Spirit of the living God, fall afresh on me. Melt me, mold me, fill me, use me." May God bless and keep you as you continue forward in your journey.

Clay